POWER & communication

ANDREW KING
Louisiana State University

WAVELAND
PRESS, INC.
Prospect Heights, Illinois

For information about this book, write or call:

Waveland Press, Inc.
P.O. Box 400
Prospect Heights, Illinois 60070
(312) 634-0081

Contents

1

Power: A Theoretical Perspective

A Theology of Power

The beginning of the human drive for power is told in the Biblical story of the Fall. Adam and Eve enjoyed effortless dominion over a benevolent nature in the Garden of Eden. Fruits fell into their hands, harvests ripened without toil, animals communed without mystery and lived together without violence. Living within the web of nature, Adam and Eve made no attempt to control, to alter, or to restructure their environment. They saw God face-to-face.

Then, they were tempted by the Serpent. This creature revealed to Adam and Eve the possibility of a new mode of existence—saying no to God and living against nature. By actively shaping nature and bending it to their will, they might become second creators and rivals of God. Adam and Eve had always said "Yes" to God and nature. In order to learn the Negative, they needed to acquire the gift from the Tree of Knowledge, Language. So, they ate the fruit of the tree, acquired human speech and, through this act of disobedience, became estranged from God and nature. In gaining the ability to say "No," human beings also shouldered the burdens of free will and moral choice.[1]

With the Fall from Grace, mankind "invented the Negative" to use the expression of the brilliant language theorist and critic, Kenneth Burke.[2] Stained by Original Sin, the human race was expelled from the Garden and

1

the long dialectic of History began.

Nature outside the Garden was often hostile and seldom predictable. Human beings faced a new curse—work. They began the long struggle against nature which gradually evolved into a transcendence of the limits of their bodies through tools. A second, manmade environment was thus imposed upon the original. They no longer apprehended the diety face-to-face. Worship became a shadow world of myth, symbol, ritual, and an arena of disputed interpretations.

Although human language brought division, it also fostered community and cooperation. Mankind set about to master the world through symbolic manipulation. Through the gift of language, man could distinguish objects by assigning them specific names. They could then be utilized in ingenious and productive combinations that had never existed in original nature. Language was a great font of power.

Language facilitated cumulative human culture. Language allowed humans to pass on the wisdom of the dead in the form of stories, sayings, and other distillations of knowledge. Words allowed people to plan for the future, to gain a precise mastery of technical operations, and to divide their labor so efficiently that complex communities were possible. Language made the world dialectical. It brought union and division simultaneously. The division of labor as a basis of social class also fostered a larger sense of unity realized in the city and the nation. The symbolic act that created the city tore apart the tribe; the civic community was rent by the nation. Human solidarity with the nation automatically affirmed estrangement from other nations. The seamless identification of the Garden was gone. Every human affirmation was also an act of negation. Every act of cooperation espoused competition with rival groups. Each act of mobilization inspired a counter-mobilization by groups beyond the pale. Language began a dialectic of history which was also an escalating dialogue of power.

The Original Sin of Language created additional problems. The capacity of human beings to imagine and to construct ideal images continually exceeded their ability to execute. They were both tormented and inspired by desires for the productions of their own imaginations—things which did not yet exist. Barely able to travel upon the land, human beings dreamed of mastering sea travel. Hardly launched upon the sea, they dreamed of flight. Once they had learned to fly, humans dreamed of transcending the limitations of the planet.

Technology, like language, represented an extension of mankind's unique ability for symbolic conceptualization. Technology allowed the human race a mastery of the great material forces, but here, as in language, the creative gift had a Janus point. Cooperation brought competition; union brought estrangement. In mastering nature, humans sometimes destroyed the balance of nature, and she struck back savagely with floods, droughts and other disasters. Matchless military organization to secure the safety of loved ones inherently transformed people into formidable killers of their own species. Even in achieving gigantic works and immense material benefits, mankind sometimes seemed in danger of becoming the tools of their tools. The dream of liberation from drudgery has a price, and freedom is accompanied by the necessity for mankind to adjust to the moral imperatives of technology.[3]

Efforts to transcend the dialectic or to retreat from it abound. History is littered with the wreckage of failed utopian experiments. The Garden exists in many disguised secular forms: the classless society of revolutionaries, the peaceable kingdom of the Quakers, or the numerous communal experiments of the 1960's. The dream of ending the dialectic of history and the ceaseless struggle between human groups will be achieved in a future Eden. There is also an Eden that is set in the past; Eden is a metaphor for childhood and lost innocence. Beyond the disenchantment and weariness of adult consciousness, the Garden beckons us to return. Yet it will be forever out of reach, much like a Currier and Ives agrarian past, the "Deserted Village" of Oliver Goldsmith, or the loving shelter of infancy.

The Quest for Meaning

Whether we assert our solidarity with others in the community or assert our individual identity against community, human beings strive for order, meaning and significance. Orientation is a powerful need. We must know where we are; we must understand the meaning of our existence. We strive to know the moral ecology of the universe. In order to enact our moral values, we must attain a certain efficacy. Our drive for understanding and identity is realized in action. We must have power to act. Our deepest values have no impact unless we operationalize them.

This world in which we seek meaning and identity is a world of power, a mobilized world. To have efficacy, we must work through its institutions, participate in its communities, appeal to others through its reigning symbols. The world is plural and speaks with many conflicting messages. To affirm one goal is to deny another, to become cathected to one group is to deny another, to embrace one set of ideas is to negate its opposite. All the while, the perceived worth and meaning of our acts and our social and political identities are being negotiated anew in the cultural and moral struggles of organized groups.

In order to control our fate, we must come to grips with the world of power. This book is to serve as a guide to the understanding of power in a modern, mobilized society. While recognizing that much power is invisible and routinized, the book treats power as a deliberate act of human organization. It deals with groups and institutions not as mere sources of potential power but as the visible consequences of power—human mobilization. Furthermore, since power is enacted, it is a relationship that is both activated and sustained by human communication. Power is a communication act. It begins as a strategic message which is formulated by a person (or group) and is addressed to an audience. The impact of the message upon the behavior of the audience has consequences that can be judged effective or ineffective, good or evil, artistic or clumsy.

Because the effects of power are complex, the book distinguishes between instrumental and symbolic uses of power.[4] Sometimes power is used to gain immediate material benefits such as jobs, money, and patronage. At other times, power confers honor, prestige, or communal deference. While instrumental and symbolic uses of power almost never exist in pure form, these distinctions yield useful insights.

Theoretical Perspective

This book rests upon two key ideas:

1.   Much power is group power. Although power seems to be exercised by individuals, they often do so as agents or "leaders" of their sponsoring groups. The power of the lone individual is an ideological and aesthetic creation.

2.   Groups are created by talk. They are begun, nurtured and even destroyed by communication. When groups are utilized as power blocks they are activated by strategically crafted discourse. It is Rhetoric (the art of persuasive communication) that builds and sustains configurations of power.

In addition, any account of the relationship between power and communication demands a theoretical perspective that includes three things:

1. An image of society;

2. A perspective on the nature of the tension between the individual and the social order;

3. A view of the role of discourse in communal life.

At present, three images or metaphors of society dominate social science. They are (1) the Integrationist Image, (2) the Conflict Image, and (3) the Negotiator Image of society. The first image highlights human cooperation and emphasizes the adjustment of the individual to the group as a central social process. The second image, Conflict, emphasizes competition as a creative force in history. It posits the world as a vast arena of warring groups. The individual and society are assumed to be implacable foes. The third image is closest to Kenneth Burke's model of dramatism. It features the idea of cooperative competition. Social cohesion is achieved through an ultimate transcendence of the competing social groups through allegiance to an over-arching social good. The Negotiator Image is a view of society in which groups appeal to one another for alliance while denigrating still other groups in an ever shifting configuration of conflict and cohesion. The central social processes are dialogue and symbolic action. Power is enhanced or neutralized through gestures of symbolic merger or division. (See Figure 1.)

The role of discourse in the Integrationist View of society is to promote stability and contentment. It would have appealed to the late Ivor Armstrong Richards who felt that the study of communication should become the search for human misunderstanding and its remedies. Those who accept an Integrationist vision of society do not believe that rhetoric should be a plaything for opportunistic individuals. Persuasion should be guided by the morality of functionalism. Responsible communication should be therapeutic—promoting individual adjustment and system maintenance for the community.

The Conflict Image of society exalts the individual. It undervalues the idea of community by emphasizing the repressive effects of institutions upon the growth of human personality. Since the fullest development of the individual is the primary objective of all social arrangements, institutions which limit individual autonomy should be cleared away like so much dead lumber. Revolutionary action on behalf of individual freedom waits like an actor in the wings.

The role of communication is as revolutionary under the Conflict view as it is conservative under the Integrationist vision. Effective communication is that which exposes the ideological nature of speech. It will unmask the hidden workings of selfish special interest under the cover of public-spirited, community-minded language. Furthermore, Conflict is a perspective that sees society as subjective in nature—a mere projection of individual wishes. It is a collective fiction. If the subjective perception of an individual can be validated by others it becomes a public or social reality.

While no single perspective of society is exhaustive, the Negotiator Image comes closest to the point of view of this book. Perspectives are like bright lights; they illuminate a portion of the landscape while they plunge the rest deeper into darkness.

All things considered, the Negotiator Image of Society appears to have greater explanatory strength than either the Conflict or the Integrationist conceptions:

1. The Negotiator conception does not idealize order as does the Integrationist vision; thus, it is better able to explain social change.

2. The Negotiator Image does not view social institutions as necessarily destructive of individual development. It is thus

Figure 1

Name of Model	Image of social integration	Image of conflict	Image of negotiation
Key Terms	Cooperation	Competition	Cooperative competition
Role of Communication	1. Root out misunderstandings 2. Gain consensus 3. Aid adjustment	1. Raise consciousness 2. Unmask special interests 3. Create social reality	Dialectical Group, class, and institutional, courtship through symbolic appeal
Ideal Society	Corporate Liberalism	Confederacy	Pluralistic Democracy
Role of Individual	Seeks like-mindedness and consensual validation	Individual as creator	Participation, action, games-man, citizen
Pathological State	Alienation	Regulation, death of motivation, client state	Destruction of the reigning symbols
World Thinkers	All functionalists	Hobbes to Sartre	Kenneth Burke

better able to analyze the human needs for order, stability, and community than the Conflict perspective.

3.   The Negotiator view suggests that human desires for individual effectiveness and social solidarity are complementary. It also posits that humans must have both "permanence and change."[6] Both experiences are vital for communities and individuals.

4.   The Negotiator Image recognizes the creative force of struggle, but it is a dialectical struggle. Because it is carried on through the manipulation of symbols, it is a struggle in which groups may compete with each other on one level, find accommodation on another level, and achieve union on a still more transcendent level. As Kenneth Burke has told us, every identification involves division and every act of division involves a compensatory act of identification. To make common cause with the Sierra Club is to set one's face against congeries of extractive industries. To embrace the principle of dictatorship automatically is to ally against the champions of republican government. President Ronald Reagan's gestures of deference to evangelical fundamentalists were sometimes seen as gestures of denigration to High Churcher's, secularists, and others who do not wholly share the fundamentalist style and ethic.

5.   The rigidity of the Integrationist Image and the brittleness of the Conflict Image simply do not reflect the dynamics of a pluralist society. A pluralist society is one in which groups struggle within a prevailing set of rules. One's status, value, and efficacy are always subject to rapid elevation or to rapid erosion. Even the rules of the game are gradually transformed; at any given time, someone's metaphor must prevail, and competition is carried on within a general framework of cultural understandings.

Relational Power

We live in a world of rank. We speak of better and worse, higher and lower, more important and less important. We constantly evaluate others. We permit, even encourage, them to evaluate us. A listener makes a judgment of the worth and potency of a speaker. Speakers craft their messages based on estimates of the significance and status of audience members. Similarly, groups attempt to change the public's perception of their worth through strategic communication.

Speakers abandon old social networks and associations in favor of upward mobility and join more prestigious linguistic communities. As a result, old groups lose their ability to frame coherent and convincing messages justifying their privileges and worth. Speakers seek wider audiences or appeal to elite groups.

Group struggles against group for access to mass media, for new recruits or for ownership of powerful symbols. Finally, groups may be displaced from high positions or abandoned by their members. Speakers are rejected by audiences. The distribution of power across society is constantly in flux. Stratification is always with us, but our place in the human hierarchy is continually being renegotiated.

Accordingly, the next several chapters will deal with power from a variety of communication contexts. Two chapters will deal with power as it is negotiated between a single speaker and his or her audience. The following chapters will deal with group power. Strategic power messages will then be considered. Finally, the role of media will be discussed.

Notes

[1]For the Fall as metaphor for the acquisition of language, I am indebted to Kenneth Burke, the founder of Dramatism and the most astute rhetorical critic of our time. His most influential works have been: *A Rhetoric of Motives* (Berkeley and Los Angeles: University of California Press, 1959); *A Grammar of Motives* (New York: Prentice-Hall, 1945); *Permanence and Change* (New York: New Republic, Inc., 1935); and *Attitudes Toward History* (Los Altos, CA: Hermes Press, 1935).

[2]For a discussion of dramatism and Burke's method of political and literary analysis, see "Interaction 111: 'Dramatism,'" ed. David L. Sills, *International Encyclopedia of the Social Sciences,* Vol. 7, 445-452.

[3]According to Ellul, "In every society there is a central motif, a chief center of interest, an undisputed assumption, a good recognized by all. It can be said, for example, that Christianity was this principal motif in the twelfth and thirteenth centuries, as was the proletarian revolution in Communist countries, the idea of the city-state in Greece of the fifth century before Christ, and technology today. The principal motif is always both ideological and material.... By a sort of tacit covenant, the members of the group undergo this moral organization and the principal motif which they approve by consensus." See Jacques Ellul, *To Will and To Do,* (Philadelphia and Boston: Pilgrim Press, 1969), p. 164.

[4]This distinction was first popularized by Murray Edelman, *The Symbolic Uses of Politics* (Urbana: University of Illinois, 1964).

[5]Ivor Armstrong Richards was impatient with what he called "the puppy war" of words. By that, he meant the emphasis on argumentation which characterized rhetorical study of his day. His study of rhetoric as a "way in which words work" is best expressed in *Philosophy of Rhetoric* (New York: Oxford University Press, 1936).

[6]Once again, I am indebted to Kenneth Burke for this concept. He argues that language itself allows us the illusion of a stable world in the midst of experiential flux.

2

The Power of the Speaker

All speakers are not created equal. Some speakers inspire stormy enthusiasm, awe, deep obedience. Others are virtually ignored or met with hostility. The power of the bond forged between speakers and audiences has been an object of speculation for centuries; it is still not fully understood.

Speaker Status

Cal Logue, a professor of Communication at the University of Georgia, has developed the concept of "speaker status."[1] According to Logue, status is the relationship of the speaker to the linguistic community: the respect, affection and trust that a speaker is accorded. Speakers exhibit visual and verbal signs that prompt their listeners to make judgments about their right to communicate. These judgments are based on many pre-message factors: the speaker's social position, economic resources, ability to reward or threaten. Similarly, one speaker may have access to public media, high-elected officials, and influential leaders, while another is confined to a narrow circle of obscure acquaintances. One speaker may enjoy membership in a distinguished family, an eminent position in a powerful organization, and an array of academic and professional credentials, while another is ignorant and isolated. It seems that every community accords to its members a larger or smaller opportunity to communicate, and a greater or lesser right to communicate on any given issue.

In addition to the pre-message and pre-textual factors that determine communicator status, characteristics of the message may modify or enhance the speaker's position. Thus, the relatively fixed factors of resources, wealth and social position may be partially overcome by performance factors. These are: situational credibility, perceived sincerity, and rhetorical skill in conveying the message. In any given situation, one or the other of these factors may be decisive. For example, Richard Nixon's status was not reduced because his expertise failed, but because he had lost his credibility as a communicator. Ronald Reagan's reputation as the Great Communicator was not enhanced by his mediocre exchanges in press conferences and lackluster performance in the first debate against Mondale in 1984. On the other hand, it was the flawless fluency and mechanical perfection of the speech of William Pitt the Younger that caused journalists like Hazlitt to question his sincerity.[2] Finally, there is always fear that the posthumous works of a novelist may jeopardize his or her place as a formidable communicator.

The remainder of this chapter will discuss many of the variables associated with Logue's concept of Speaker Status. Additionally, it will include some that transcend social class and individual skill.

Visual Grammar

The Formal Setting: Anyone who has seen an angry mob silence an orator knows what a fragile and artificial convention public speaking is. It is a form of communication that makes tremendous demands upon an audience; it demands sustained attention, and it limits audience response to gross displays of approval and disapproval. Special architecture and technology combine to increase the speaker's control over the audience. Raised platforms, tiered seats, converging sight-lines, microphones, lighting, visual aids, slides, screens and special graphics have all enhanced a modern speaker's power to capture and hold attention.[3]

Earlier in this century, fascist and communist dictators magnified the traditional speaker's rally to Wagnerian proportions. Smoking torches, sweeping search lights, massed flags, rehearsed chants, and a vast choreography of the masses lifted the speaker to godlike heights. As crowds chanted "Duce! Duce!" or "Seig Heil!" electronic devices captured the mesmeric sounds and fed them back in a series of crashing ocean waves.

More recently, Max Atkinson[4] has studied the power conventions of more ordinary speaker settings. After careful review of the films and videotapes of hundreds of political speakers, Atkinson has come to the conclusion that a speaker's mastery of an audience is actually a simpler matter than the ancient students of oratory believed. The classical rhetorics of Aristotle, Cicero, Quintilianus and others formed a complex body of precepts. Persuasive oratory was the art of arts, and a lifetime of practice was needed to attain the subtle understanding of how to master an audience, to mold it like hot wax, to breath soft dreams into its soul.

Atkinson affirms that his precepts are far fewer and rather more potent than the subtle insinuations and tortured strategies of traditional rhetoric. First, an orator's control over an audience is greatly enhanced by an understanding of a few customary patterns of audience behavior. Secondly, audience responses are elicited by aesthetic form rather than logical content.

According to Atkinson, speakers routinely evoke applause when they engage in praise and blame, mount climactic introductions, use lists of three, and recite binary contrasts. Every politician is expected to praise the loyalists and denigrate the opposition. Whether the success of this form is based on tribal need for identity or mere ritual convention is moot; the ancient formula for audience participation has been popular since Aristotle observed that it was never difficult to praise Athens to Athenians. Audiences have been trained to respond to introductions since childhood. Lists of three (Churchill's "blood, sweat and tears" or MacArthur's "duty, honor, country"), and contrasting pairs locked into parallel structures (Martin Luther King's "Our long hot summers are the product of our winters of neglect") are rhetorical commonplaces.

Books on oratory have admonished the speaker to maintain eye contact with the audience in order to engender a lively sense of communication. Atkinson decries another function, that of keeping the audience under "surveillance."[5] Public speaking makes much greater demands on a listener's attention than does ordinary conversation, thus scrutinizing an audience reduces the chances that they will read newspapers, talk to one another, or wander off.

Socialization to Authority

Some public roles command deference and attention. This deference is learned; it is a part of early socialization. For example, a medical doctor enjoys a certain license to do things that would be denied to one's most intimate friends. Upon entering an examination room, a patient is routinely told to "take off your clothes" and get up on the table. Most do so without hesitation; the origin of this compliance lies in childhood. When the child was first asked to strip at the age of three, he or she may have balked, full of fear and resentment. The parents chided: "It's okay, honey. This is the *Doctor*." By age sixteen, such obedience had become utterly routine.

Of course, a doctor-patient relationship is hedged about with specific limitations and responsibilities. Yet, it is always available in times of crisis.

An Indian doctor described its potency to me:

> I do not know how it is in the United States for I have never practiced here, but a dying patient in many parts of the world is a dangerous being, a focus of family pilgrimage. Relatives who have not been seen for twenty years appear to observe the final release of the spirit. As the hour of death nears, doctors are sometimes reproached for being negligent. They are reviled for not having done enough to save Kalid's life. At such time the doctor may be able to avoid an ugly business only to the extent that he can treat his attackers as patients. He may assure them that they are strangely upset because they are ill. Moreover, he will note that they are flushed, full of fever, and that he must really give them a pill to make them feel better. At the very least they must return home to rest. In this way even the most violent individual is made cooperative, respectful, even timid. [6]

Thus, the most rudimentary cue may evoke the doctor-patient role. The childhood pattern of obedience is enacted.

The paradigm of institutionalized compliance is found throughout social life. In the "Information Society," nearly everyone is dependent upon the authority of experts. The ordinary citizen does not arise in the morning to kill, as well as cook, his or her own food. Citizens do not educate their young, build their own shelters, manufacture their own amusements, craft their own art, heal their own bodies, and prescribe their own forms of religious worship. A specialized person is a dependent person.

In order to retain its own power, professionalism is strongly hedged about. A doctor is not allowed to raise taxes or declare war, only to heal people. Even that limited license is fragile. A gradual loss of confidence means a withdrawal of privilege. Professions such as teaching have not been undermined by firebrands, but by a gradual loss of public confidence. They have lost what Richard Sennett has named autonomy, the right to define a situation within a carefully bounded domain. The public has reasserted its right to define the nature of the educational problem and the nature of its solution.

According to Bertrand Russell,[7] the rise of the expert coincided with the decline of the intellectual, the spiritual descendant of the priest, whom "education has robbed" of "his power." Russell maintained that mass education has demystified the sacred books, narrowed the intellectual's mandate, and replaced wisdom with mere information.

For certain roles, the culture transmits images of autonomy and power. For others, it transmits images of lack of self-control and dependency. Certain groups are expected to be deviant and rewarded for being so. When a drug addict is caught, his treatment is savage repression. There is an expectation that he will steal to support his habit, thus becoming even more deviant (criminal).[8]

Of course, it is crucial that the deviant accept the label given to him by dominant groups and cooperate by embracing his subordinate role. Those who do not admit to deviance do not exhibit guilt or illness or incapacitation when they are caught and publically labeled. Robert Lifton[9] has pointed out that soldiers who refused to accept classifications of illness continued to function. On the other hand, once they accepted a classification of disturbance, they deteriorated rapidly.

Height and Power

Susan Lee Bernstein,[10] in her 1985 study "Height and Power," notes that vertical dominance is practiced throughout society. During the Ford-Carter presidential debates of 1976, Carter is said to have asked for a four-inch platform so that his five feet nine-inch frame would appear roughly equal to Gerald Ford's six feet one-inch body. Bernstein noted that "a woman selling Tupperware is told to elevate the product and look at it with reverence."[11] She reminded us that judges' desks are raised, that European imperial and honor guards are generally composed of exceptionally tall soldiers, and that a major movie star's studio advertised him as 6'2" when he was only 5'9½".

Bernstein discovered that height is a dialectical term. There is no absolute tallness or shortness, highness or lowness. The relative value of a given height is determined by its context. Persons over 6 feet 7 inches experience the same feelings of rejection experienced by those under 5 feet. They are no longer tall in a socially acceptable way.

Bernstein notes that "the comical example of height = power" is portrayed in Charlie Chaplin's film *The Great Dictator.* Hitler and Mussolini try to outdo each other by jacking their barbershop chairs higher and higher into the sky.

Bernstein's study catalogs the vertical dominance of animal struggles (the victor stands over the victim), the tribal expressions of subordination through groveling, kneeling before King or religious officers, the elevation of the victor in battle, and the symbols of high and low to denote good and evil or sacred and secular in religion. She notes the visual grammar of art, particularly religious art: the Gods are in the high places or mountains and "in the scenes of the Nativity Jesus is the central powerful figure. To emphasize this the three kings are usually shown bowing or otherwise prostrating themselves."[12]

The equation of height with power is easily and unconsciously made. For example, in 1985, I asked several classes to estimate the heights of Ronald Reagan and George Bush. A large majority thought Reagan slightly taller (approx. 6'2" to the vice-president's 6'1"). Bush is, in fact, substantially taller (6'3" to Reagan's 6'1").

Bernstein administered a similar, but much more comprehensive, test to a large group of university students. She asked them to estimate the physical stature of world leaders and rock stars. With the exception of the late Chairman Mao, most students overestimated the heights of world leaders by substantial margins. Prime Minister Thatcher was thought to be fully three inches taller than Queen Elizabeth. She is slightly shorter.

A body of research in non-verbal communication suggests that persons automatically ascribe greater height to persons of higher status.[13] Speigel and Machotka[14] found that, in drawings, individuals in more expansive poses (greater height, raised heads) were seen as more powerful than persons who appeared smaller or were in more constricted stances.

The body-builder Arnold Schwartzenegger noted that judges had a strong tendency to award the physique contest to the taller man, despite the greater impression of bulk and strength that shorter body-builders may achieve.[15]

In my judgment, "heightism" has little to do with the belief that taller persons are more credible because they are more able to carry out their threats. The bias is deeply embedded in the visual grammar of western civilization. For a speaker, it has functional advantages. The elevation of the speaker gives him or her a much larger field of vision. Elevation gathers and keeps attention. In appropriate circumstances, it may awaken associations of obedience, even veneration, which are as deep as the roots of human community.

Language and Power

During the late 1950's, Alan C. Ross published an article called "U or Non-U, An Essay in Sociological Linguistics."[16] According to Ross, the relative power of a speaker in Britain is cued by language. Ross argues that certain word choices are expressive hallmarks of social position. By choice, Ross means a rhetorical choice, a particular stylistic selection among an array of words that mean nearly the same thing. He found that U (Upper Class speakers) said "wireless," while non-U speakers said "radio," "Jam" instead of "preserve," "sick" rather than "ill," and so on.[17] In addition to the vocabulary differences, there were the differences in melodic line (the musical 62 phonemes of West Country speech to the 50 of the "posh" southern English standard).

The association of language with power has a vast folklore. For many years, it has been a convention of theatre and film that powerful people spoke slowly while powerless speakers (petty criminals, social climbers, impressarios of questionable enterprises) spoke rapidly. The powerful speakers knew that everyone would hang upon their words, while the subordinate persons blurted out their messages hastily in order to get a word in edgewise to people who seemed little interested in anything they had to say. Within the past fifteen years, researchers have produced evidence for the belief that powerful persons talk more than others in social groups[18] and that they take more turns.[19] Others have found talkativeness or sheer volume of talking within a group correlated with judgments of potency and effectiveness.[20]

In the early 1960's, Basil Bernstein[21] asserted that speech patterns not only restrict upward mobility of particular individuals, but also that they tend to limit the social, political, economic, and intellectual opportunities of large groups. Bernstein conceptualizes power in class terms. For him, classes are power groupings relatively fixed by birth and early socialization. The most important aspect of the early socialization is the acquisition of a language, and it is this variety of language that determines consciousness. Although mobility is possible for individuals, the status of most speakers is maintained by the consciousness (perspective of the world) expressed and maintained by a set of verbal habits.

Bernstein reduces these sets to two which he names *elaborated* and *restricted* codes, roughly corresponding to middle- and lower-class groupings in Britain. These codes were forms of address through which the weaker class unwittingly reinforced its own powerflesness. The dominant groups used a universalistic perspective to exert a measure of control over the world of people and things. The codes had mighty consequences for their users. They maintained a stable view of the world, a problem-solving style, a characteristic vocabulary, and a role set.

According to Bernstein, the speakers of the restricted codes use a limited concrete vocabulary, little qualification or generalization, and short predictable sentences. On the other hand, the speakers of the elaborated code use high levels of generalization, a sophisticated degree of conceptualization, much qualification, and sentences that are both grammatically and logically complex.

Because of their universalistic perspective, the elaborated speakers are able to entertain a variety of life scenarios and to transcend the tribal and parochial perspective of the speakers of the restricted code. The restricted code speakers are blocked into tribal patterns of response: passivity and resignation, rejection and violence. Thus, the elaborated speaker's view, in opposition to that of the restricted speaker, is sacred versus secular, that of an insider versus an outsider. The restricted speaker is not able to deal with the elaborated speaker on an egalitarian basis of argument and debate, but is limited to threats, pleas, or surrender of the initiative. The style of the elaborated code is one of negotiation and of the personal assumption of responsibility.

While the effect of the class system is to limit access to elaborated codes that would give the speaker "access to the grounds of his socialization"[22] and a greater understanding of the social order, people do change their speech habits and rise in the social order. The linguistic variability of the self-made is a commonplace. Everyone knows of the code-switcher who, like Natty Bumpo, speaks like a sage one moment and a repossessor of automobiles the next.[23] The study of newspapers is most instructive in this regard. The so-called non-U (non-Upper Class) newspaper begins as a war monger sheet, reeking with hatred of foreigners, full of hostility and paranoia. It is consolidated with another local sheet and makes a bid for an upscale audience. Gradually, it tries to meld the old and new readership, becoming ever less dogmatic; its standards of evidence become more rigorous, its outlook more balanced. Instead of speaking only in local terms, it gains a national, even an international perspective. It becomes ever more bland, more secular, more relativistic. No longer able to find red meat and the gossip of the local gods, its old readership deserts it for the telly and the pub.

This is not to say that there are not many admirable features of a restricted code speech. According to Bernstein, such speech is orientated toward immediate present, but this very blindness to an array of alternative and relativistic solutions has substantial psychological benefits. Its frame of reference is that of the tribe; it absolves its members of the terrible burdens of individual responsibility, and does not celebrate the disorientation and sense of alienation that are the lot of the upwardly mobile. While the elaborated code newspapers, the *New York Times* or the *London Times,* celebrate a belief in rationality, science, and technology, the restricted code paper presents the world as a kind of fantasy revenge. It makes sense of the world by showing the rich and powerful as corrupt, venal, and unhappy; it plays upon a paranoid and conspiratorial sense of reality, a deep fear of loss of control, the displacement of human agents by machines. It makes harsh social comparisons that imply an absolute moral order, whereas the elaborated papers engage in hermeneutic struggles. They view the world as a clash of paradigms, and inculcate a sense of guilt and the necessity for constant negotiation and accommodation. The elaborated papers are grounded in appeals to the modern, secular, relativistic, interdependent, complex, and cosmopolitan elements in society. Their paradigm is the enthymeme, a parade of premises, evidence, conclusions and qualifications. In contrast, the restricted paradigm is the narrative, the communal drama.

The bias of intelligence tests toward a command of the dominant idiom is well-known. Similarly, the association of fluency with intelligence is deeply embedded in the popular culture. Michael Knox[24] notes that English exchange students in American Engineering programs were rated higher in intelligence, personal effectiveness, and competence than their American counterparts of roughly similar achievement. After an analysis of writing samples and oral interviews, Knox concluded that the English students differed only in their speech and writing skills.

The connection between social power and language is well-understood. As Karl Deutsch[25] has taught us, language, rather than ethnicity, is the chief determinant of nationhood. Whatever one may say about linguistic tolerance in bilingual nations like Belgium and Canada, few will maintain that such diversity makes them stronger, more orderly, or more cohesive. The loud debates over Black English and Spanish in the United States, Welsh in Britain, French in Canada, Breton in France, and German in the Tyrol are struggles over community control.

Non-Verbal Power

During the past decade, an enormous body of research documented the influence of non-verbal behaviors in communication. Since 1971, when Mehrabian[26] concluded that 93% of generalized meaning could be attributed to non-verbal messages and, again, in 1972[27], when he noted that 65% of social meaning in face-to-face communication is transmitted by means of non-verbal messages, a niagara of research has established the significant role of the extraverbal domain.

The appreciation of the visual grammar of power has had a varied history. Aristotle was impressed with the power of signs and visual verification in both his *Rhetoric* and *Poetics*. The subject has always been one of controversy. During the nineteenth century, while Carlyle discoursed on the importance of clothes as signs of authority, John Stuart Mill affirmed that all "real" experience could be expressed in logical verbal declaration, and those things which could not be so expressed were mere phantoms.

The non-verbal dimension of power is expressed in objects, in relational behavior, and in the deliberate manipulation of symbols. Asa Berger[28] reminds us that the amassed books in a lawyer's office suggest that knowledge is power, that a digital watch suggests modernity and efficacy, that clutter suggests weakness and spaciousness power.

Studies in eye contact demonstrate the complicated relationship between power and gaze behavior. For decades, Raymond Birdwhistell maintained that direct gaze was the badge of the powerful; indirect or furtive gaze was the mark of the subordinate. According to Birdwhistell, the penetrating gaze of the dominant individual is a behavior indicating territorial invasion. Other research found that prolonged eye contact communicated low status. Martin Remland[29] resolves this inconsistency by pointing out the situational nature of gaze behavior dominance. The eye contact of the dominant figure is a part of a constellation of dominant behaviors. Remland notes that dominant and subordinate persons "interact in ways that punctuate their status"[30] in a group or organization. Powerful people are more relaxed than their subordinates, less attentive to the communication of others, more expansive, more invading of the space of others, less vulnerable to spatial invasion, more in control of floor space. In addition, Remland tells us they are less frequently interrupted, take more turns in conversation, talk more of the time, and are touched less often. In summary, the measure of speaker power is the degree of control over the entire interactive process.

Gender and Power

The vast literature on the subject of the relation of gender to power is, for the most part, strategic; that is, its function was to make a contribution to sexual politics. The long debate over the origins of male dominance is beyond our scope here. The debate over whether sexual differences were biological or cultural created mythologies of gender during the 1970's which were bewildering in their complexity, number, and hermeneutic brilliance.

Much of the research of the late 1970's and 1980's has come from the setting of the business organization. Studies conducted during the 1970's[31] confirm that women get lower starting salaries than men and are given fewer opportunities for personal development and job advancement. In a 1983 study, however, Ellen M. Murray[32] examines the perceived opportunities for job advancement in relation to employee sex and fails to find significant differences. Other studies indicate that women tend to be isolated from important sources of information and are shuttled into dead-end jobs more often than men.[33] Still other studies indicate that women lack a long-term power perspective that allows them to advance within organizations. The causes of the special problems women face in business are related to history, structure, and culture.

The relationships of these disadvantages to language use are less clear. While feminist writers have suggested that men and women inhabit different worlds (male versus female consciousness), no firm consensus has emerged as to the role played by language in this matter.

To be sure, a stereotypical pattern of "male speech" or "power speech" exists. Male language is said to reflect an instrumental perspective, self-confidence, persistence and independence. Female language is said to reflect an expressive dimension—supportive, emotional and dependent.[34] Until the middle of the 1960's, women's magazines endorsed the values of the female communication model as being more humane than those of the male model. The denigration of the women's model began in the late 1960's, and the single admired model became that of male speech. A recent study by Barbatsis, Wong and Herek[35] demonstrates the extent of the change that had taken place. While earlier studies of mass media and films demonstrate the presence of both male and female speech models during the 1970's, the Barbatsis, Wong and Herek study shows the traditional male model firmly in the saddle for the speech of characters of both sexes. Their survey of television drama shows "the predominant model of interpersonal interaction for both male and female characters was a dominant male style of interaction resulting in the portrayal of a struggle for dominance."[36]

In his study of manners and power, Jordan[37] does not find a correlation between traditional male speech ("containing a preponderence of messages attempting to assert control") and the achievement of power in a group setting. According to Jordan, several U.S. presidents equated tough talk (strong language denoting violence, war and mutilation) with masculinity. Jordan found that a mannerly style of discourse (indirect approach, elaborate preface, expressions of respect and concern) was far more persuasive for subordinates and at least as persuasive for dominant people in confrontative situations. One suspects that, in the American South, the bone-crushing style is even less effective. Tough talk has the disadvantage of being perceived as a compensation for weakness or a cover for deep insecurity. The case for the effectiveness of good manners was made as long ago as Castiglione's *Courtier.*[38]

Notes

[1]Cal Logue has presented this idea in its fullness at several scholarly forums as professor of Speech Communication at the Department of Speech Communication, University of Georgia, Athens, Georgia 30602.

[2]Floyd Douglas Anderson and Andrew A. King, "William Hazlitt as a Critic of Parliamentary Speaking," *Quarterly Journal of Speech,* 67 (1981), 52.

[3]See Charles Merriam, "The Miranda of Power," in *The Rhetoric of Non-verbal Communication,* ed. Haig A. Bosmajian (Glenview: Scott, Foresman and Co., 1971), p. 112.

[4]Max Atkinson, *Our Master's Voices: The Language and Body Language of Politics* (London: Methuen and Co., 1984).

[5]Ibid., p. 12.

[6]Conversation with Secundra Jains, M.D., SCA Convention, Palmer House, 8 November 1984.

[7]Bertrand Russell, *Power: A New Social Analysis* (New York: W.W. Norton Co., 1938), p. 43.

[8]See Joseph P. Gusfield, "A Dramatistic Theory of Status Politics," in *The Collective Definition of Deviance,* ed. F. James Davis and Richard Stivers (New York: Free Press, 1975), pp. 24-39.

[9]Robert Jay Lifton, *Home From the War* (New York: Simon and Schuster, 1973) (esp. Chap. 13), and also "Labelling Theory Reconsidered," in Howard S. Becker, *Outsiders* (New York: Free Press, 1973), pp. 176-208.

[10]Susan Lisa Bernstein, "Height and Power" (University of Arizona, Tucson, AZ: unpubl., 1985).

[11]Ibid.

[12]Ibid.

[13]See Ralph Keyes, *The Height of Your Life* (Boston: Little, Brown and Co., 1980), and also N.M. Henley, *Body Politics: Sex, Power and Non-Verbal Communication* (Englewood Cliffs, New York: Prentice-Hall, 1977).

[14]J.P. Speigel and P. Machota, *Messages of the Body* (New York: The Free Press, 1974).

[15]Charles Gaines and George Butler, *Pumping Iron* (New York: Simon and Schuster, 1977). Arnold is quoted on these matters throughout Chapter 7.

[16]Alan S.C. Ross, "U and Non-U: An Essay in Sociological Linguistics," in *New Rhetorics,* ed. Martin Steinman (New York: Scribners, 1970), pp. 227-248.

[17] Ibid., p. 229.

[18] Robert F. Bales, *Personality and Interpersonal Behavior* (New York: Holt, Rinehart and Winston, 1970).

[19] B. Eakins and R.G. Eakins, *Sex Differences in Human Communication* (Boston: Houghton-Mifflin, 1978).

[20] C.L. Kleinke, M. Kahn and T. Tully, "First Impressions of Talking Rates in Opposite-Sex and Same-Sex Interactions," *Social Behavior and Personality,* 7 (1979): 81-91.

[21] Basil Bernstein, *Class, Codes and Control* (London and Boston: Routledge and Kegan Paul, 1981), pp. 38-39.

[22] Ibid., p. 176.

[23] This verbal virtuosity is probably characteristic of marginal status.

[24] Michael Knox, *Fluency and Apparent Intelligence* (University of Bristol, United Kingdom: unpubl., 1984).

[25] Karl Deutsch, *Nationalism and Social Communication: An Inquiry into the Foundations of Nationality* (Cambridge, MA: M.I.T. Press, 1966), pp. 41-45.

[26] A Mehrabian, "A Verbal and Nonverbal Interaction of Strangers in a Waiting Situation," *Journal of Experimental Research in Personality,* 6 (1976): 127-138.

[27] A. Mehrabian, *Nonverbal Communication* (Chicago: Aldine and Atherton, 1972).

[28] Asa Arthur Berger, *Signs in Contemporary Culture* (New York: Longmans, 1981), see Chap. 4.

[29] Martin Remland, "Superior-Subordinate Interaction," *Communication Quarterly,* 32 (Winter 1984), 43.

[30] Ibid.

[31] M. Heilman and L. Saruwatari, "When Beauty is Beastly: The Effects of Appearance and Sex on Evaluations of Job Applicants for Managerial and Non-Managerial Jobs," *Organizational Behavior and Human Performance,* 23(1979):372.

[33] Ibid., 156.

[34] For a brilliant exposition of these matters, see Noelle Bisseret Moreau, "Education, Ideology and Class/Sex Identity," in *Language and Power,* ed. Cheris Kramarae, Muriel Schulz and William M. O'Barr (Beverly Hills: Sage, 1984), pp. 43-61. I further believe that one could document the change through a study of the major women's mass circulation magazines between 1960 and 1980.

[35] Gretchen S. Barbatsis, Martin R. Wong and Gregory M. Herek, "A Struggle for Dominance: Relational Communication Patterns in Television Drama," *Communication Quarterly,* 31 (Spring 1983), 148-155.

[36] Ibid., 148.

[37] Paul Felix Jordan, *What the Rich and the Powerful Have to Say About Manners* (University of Minnesota, Minneapolis, MN: 1986).

[38] Baldassare Castiglione wrote *The Book of the Courtier,* a work describing the conversations that took place at the Court of the Duke of Urbino in 1507. A modern reader may be struck at its close resemblance to modern self-improvement books. George Bill translation (Penguin Books, 1967) with notes is best.

3

The Power of the Audience

The power of the great speaker is an illusion. The speaker's power is granted by the audience. The audience is many. The speaker is one. The speaker is weak. The audience is strong. The conventions of public speaking are fragile. Anyone who has seen a mob audience turn and take charge of an event knows this well.

Of course, there are the many testimonials of fascist dictators that audiences are cowardly, that they yearn for a leader, or that they wish only to be mastered, seduced and ordered about. One ought to remember the kinds of audiences that the fascists addressed. They were frightened people whose nations had gone bankrupt, whose social structures and institutions had been crushed, and whose hopes and plans had been blasted. These desperate, charisma-prone audiences would have embraced anyone who promised to deliver them from terror and oblivion.

The seduction model of persuasion is inappropriate for the Anglo-American audience. As Michael McGee[1] points out, the "people" is not a mere aggregate, but a group held together by a consciousness of a common destiny and a revolutionary past. The old puritan model of governance, "to be with one another rather than to be over one another," is still alive in egalitarian models of communication. As Hugh Duncan[2] notes, we follow our superiors, we order our inferiors, but we argue and debate with those who are our equals; hence American political rhetoric bristles with anti-authoritarian appeals. "Equality of opportunity" is a phrase upon which debate has been adjourned. Discussions of hierarchy and class in America produce great tension and must be hedged about with all sorts of euphemism and disclaimer.

Withholding Power

As Richard Newbold Adams observes, a leader's power comes from below, from the aggregate of resources and skills represented by his or her audience. He further argues that, in a complex, pluralistic society, allocated power may come to be seen as "indistinguishable from the direct exercise of power."[3] Although people prefer participation, they may decide to withdraw their allocated power from a government. French Canadians, Basques, South African Blacks, and both Protestant and Catholic Ulstermen have shown that it is possible to withdraw a considerable part of their delegated power.

According to Jurgen Habermas[4], many groups and institutions are vulnerable to this kind of action on the part of their constituent audiences. Institutions such as capitalism and representative democracy lack legitimacy. They face a legitimation crisis because their constituent groups have not discussed these institutions and come to a consensus about their function, worth and meaning. Habermas believes that all of our inherited institutions must be the subject of intense public discussion. Only public participation and reformulation can restore their legitimacy.

The speaker must remember that power is reciprocal. It must be exercised according to the nature and situation of "the other." In an egalitarian environment, the speaker who asks for power does so on the grounds the request is made on the audience's behalf, that it is merely temporary, and that the allocation is justified by the speaker's merit. Every moral order comes to grips with power in its own way: socialism does so by income redistribution; technocracy on the grounds that it empowers the whole society; capitalism on the grounds that its inequalities are generated by merit. The speaker must respect the ideological pieties of his or her audience.

The Audience Empowers the Speaker

During the 1960's, popular movements brought a renaissance of the art of public speaking. Surprisingly, speakers who were tired, dispirited and taciturn were almost instantly pumped up by their audiences. Black preachers stood before audiences who bathed them in affection, support, validation, veneration, and faith. During the course of my research on communication in the civil rights movement, I was given the opportunity to address several of these audiences. I remember being overwhelmed by the antiphonal responses my remarks evoked and the flood of warm approval. Another white academic, John Dollard, also found his dry prose becoming clothed in thunder before the rural southern audiences he addressed a generation earlier.[5] The constant feedback of inspirational response was difficult to resist. I became eloquent because the audience certified my eloquence.

The speaker wishing to unify an audience can always build a certain amount of audience response from the ground up. Ronald Reagan's 1976 primary campaign in New Hampshire was instructive in this regard. Even before the most sluggish audiences, Reagan responded to laughter or puzzlement with vigorous head nods. He acknowledged the behavior just as if the listener had spoken. Reagan began by speaking directly to the individual and in mid-sentence would turn to share his reaction with the audience, thus making the response *their* common property. This reward gave the audience permission for a still larger response. Soon, he had the whole group responding like a trained chorus.

Empowering the Audience

In a curious turnabout, the speaker may also empower the audience. This is particularly so if the speaker represents a social movement, a religious group, or any organization whose aims appear to be in tension with those of the larger society. As J. Burdick and Gordon Johns[6] note, joining a movement not only gives power to the leadership, but also to the rank and file. For example, they point out that the act of joining the Pentecostal Church in Mexico allows peasants to break other traditional patterns. They are more likely than others to adopt new patterns of agriculture, consumption, etc. Similarly, the Huguenots in France became innovators in many areas, pioneering new industries and economic arrangements, and importing ideas from abroad. Further, Burdick and Johns point out, a movement gives to its constituency a language in which its new experiences may be expressed.[7] This is the so-called party line, the cluster of clichés that distress outsiders who may partly agree with the beliefs of the movement but are repelled by the threadbare slogans and tired shibboleths in which these beliefs are couched. As Burdick and Johns note, the patterned and ritualistic responses of movements have many functions:

1. They provide ready answers for outsiders and members of the established order who may oppose the movement;
2. They provide a cognitive structure in which further change may take place;
3. They provide a codification for beliefs and experiences that were hitherto inaccessible or ineffable;

4. They give the individual a sense of personal power and control over his or her own world (despite the deep fatalism in which many movements speak).

Everyone who has ever served in the Army notes the moment when a young man proclaims himself a soldier. It is a moment in which the sergeant's clichés, which only yesterday had seemed a meaningless argot, suddenly spring to life and seem to express the deepest aspirations of his soul. The peculiar slogans are suddenly real.

It is at this juncture that I must question the belief of Habermas. Habermas believes that institutions can be made legitimate through consciousness-raising, by "seeing through" their ideological weaknesses, and by unremitting critical reflection. This cognitive participation on the part of ordinary people will bring loyalty and commitment, in a word, *power*, to the institutions. In my opinion, the troop indoctrination sessions, in which soldiers were free to question the meanings of patriotic symbols and in which the origins of their powers were made clear, actually eroded social cohesion and patriotism. Young men who were gung-ho soldiers began to speak of the arbitrariness of national loyalty, of the accidents of group membership, etc. The kind of participation that ensures loyalty is group action in which one does not indulge in the luxury of critical reflection. It is experiential, but not analytic. Far from destroying a sense of individual worth, such commitment actually empowers the individual to take the initiative. It enables him or her to endure deep physical pain and to survive crushing setbacks.

Asking for a Mandate

Speakers and leaders who ask their constituencies for a little will get a little; speakers who ask for much will get much. Bill Budenholzer's[8] study of public campaigns is instructive in this regard. He concludes that those campaigns that ask for too little are in great danger of being dismissed as trivial.

He tells stories of respondents who, when asked by their alumni associations for "just a single dollar per month — only twelve dollars per year," laughed with contempt and threw the request away. There is a belief that one should not make the barriers to persuasion too high and that one way to reduce them is not to ask for very much. Messages are sugar-coated, full of expressions of ease and convenience. This is a sensible strategy for a mere commercial transaction, but it does nothing to empower the maker of such messages. In fact, it assures that responses will be episodic and weak. As Budenholzer points out, the more serious the matter, one needs to ask for more, and hence, one is likely to get more. Churchill said: "I have never promised anything but blood, tears, toil and sweat" and he mobilized a nation. Budenholzer includes some rather extreme cases of commitment, even copies of Vietcong recruitment messages in his study. These messages ask for everything. They promise suffering, violent death, torture, poverty. They envision a life in which family is forsaken, friends left behind. They promise a life where one is cursed, reviled, hunted, and ultimately sacrificed. Thousands of youth surged forth, eager for this sacrifice. Suddenly, their lives were charged with meaning, and they were living more swiftly and keenly than ever before.

It is noteworthy that their accounts of this conversion experience paralleled those of the lives of medieval saints.[9] Initially, they wandered in confusion and disorientation; then came revelation, accompanied by vertigo and a blinding flash (almost always it was a moment of illumination). A feeling of great inner strength followed. There was also knowledge, and a commitment to a new way of life. A similar narrative is found in the life of a philosopher like Rousseau, or a scientist like Darwin. It is almost as if they had been empowered by the majesty of the narrative. No doubt there are many such narratives. Some are stories of dependence and weakness, others of autonomy and power. All are available as basic human stories, yet always experienced anew — as individual and unprecedented.

Conclusion

Despite the stories of charismatic power and superhuman speakers, it is apparent that, at least for the vast majority of speakers, the locus of power is the audience. The audience may refuse to mobilize its power, to withhold its power, or to extend its mandate to a spokesman. The nature of the terms and the size of the mandate are hedged about by circumstances, culture, and the audacity of the speaker.

Notes

[1] Michael Calvin McGee, "In Search of the People: A Rhetorical Alternative," *Quarterly Journal of Speech,* 61 (1975), 235-49.

[2] Hugh D. Duncan, *Communication and Social Order* (New York: Bedminister Press, 1962), p. 298.

[3] Richard Newbold Adams, *Energy and Structure: A Theory of Social Power* (Austin, TX: University of Texas Press, 1975), p. 45.

[4] Jurgen Habermas, "Hannah Arendt's Communications Conception of Power," *Social Research,* 44 (1977), 3. See also Habermas, "Toward a Theory of Communication Competence," in *Recent Sociology, No. 2: Patterns of Communication Behavior,* ed. H.P. Drietzel (London: Macmillan, 1970), p. 369. See also Donald P. Cushman and David Dietrich, "A Critical Reconstruction of Jurgen Habermas'

Holistic Approach as Social Philosopher," *Journal of the American Forensic Association,* 26 (1979), 135-136.

[5]John Dollard, *Caste and Class in A Southern Town* (New York: Doubleday, 1957), pp. 242-243.

[6]James Burdick and Gordon Johns, *Empowerment and the Act of Joining* (University of Toronto: unpubl., 1986).

[7]Ibid., p. 48.

[8]Bill Budenholzer, *The Making of a Movement* (Tucson, AZ: unpubl., 1985). See also Hans Toch, *The Social Psychology of Social Movements* (New York: Bobbs Merrill, 1965).

[9]The distinguished scholar of narrative theory and French literature, Ross Chandler, gave me the insight about the similarity of the enlightenment experience as a rite of passage among a great many sacred and secular groups.

4

Power Strategies

The notion of strategy is of military origin. Originally, it designated a plan for outwitting and defeating an enemy with the least cost to one's own forces. In communication, strategy is thought of as a message that serves as a symbolic substitute for violence. The term retains its connotations of attack and defense, despite the fact that strategy in communication may win battles that are more symbolic than material in their final outcome. .

Strategy is embodied in messages. It is communication to an opponent by means of mutually shared symbols. This process of sending effective messages as a means of avoiding violent confrontation occurs even in the animal world. The erection of quills or fur to increase perceived body size, the roar of the lion, and the stormy dances of alpha chimps are all messages of intimidation.

The literature of warfare is full of advice about the strategic military message. Clausewitz preferred the symbolic threat of force to open struggle. Even today, strategic stockpiles of weapons are used as symbolic threats. The theory behind the arms race is that nuclear weapons are so terrible that they will never have to be used. The flaw in this strategy is that, if opponents truly come to believe that a weapon is far too monstrous to be used under any circumstances, the threat loses its deterrent effect. Thus, messages sent by making and stockpiling these weapons lose credibility. Messages lacking in credibility signal weakness rather than power.

The term strategy may be defined as an efficacious pattern of behavior cast in the form of a set of verbal or visual messages. These efficacious patterns represent a kind of geometry of forms—ideal relationships that place one in a decisive position of influence during an adversary situation. Strategies are not real; they are mental constructs—general forms that have been abstracted from thousands of years of human struggle. They are roughly analogous to molds, jars, or metal castings into which materials are poured to be shaped into various configurations. Perhaps a better analogy is a mathematical formula which can be applied to a variety of problems and assigned many different values.

The relationship between strategy and message is that of general to particular, species to individual, abstract function to concrete realization. For example, a general strategy which is ethically questionable but highly effective is sometimes called "guilt by association" or, still more commonly, "birds of a feather flock together." This general strategy might be embodied in a particular message: a doctored photograph of a well-known politician surrounded by fascists, communists or other pariahs. Mere physical proximity is taken for ideological identity. The effectiveness of this message would be determined by the nature of the viewing audience, the moral and political climate of the time, recent events, the credibility of the message source and of the particular politician being slandered, etc.

The systematic use of messages as a means of attack and defense was pioneered in the law courts of Ancient Greece. Very early in the fifth century B.C., two Greek Syracusans, Corax and Tisias, wrote the first manual on Rhetoric, the art of persuasion. Nothing remains of this manual except for references in other surviving works of the Hellenic era. Socrates tells us that their primary strategy was that of probability;[1] i.e., the selection and presentation of all of the most conventionally accepted appearances of guilt or innocence before a jury. For example, Corax advised anyone accused of robbing a larger person to plead, in effect: "Is it probable that a wormy crestfallen cipher like me would even think of accosting a huge heavily muscular individual like that? Not very likely." Since procedures involving written evidence, documents, and other kinds of "inartistic proof"[2] were not well-developed, and, since juries may have numbered as many as five hundred people, it is not inconceivable that a strategy of employing conventional stereotypes may have been widely used and very often effective.

Called Rhetoric, this art of mobilizing public opinion on one's behalf was rapidly extended beyond the law courts to the assemblies and governing phyles. It became the general art of discourse, both written and spoken. Its modern revival in the universities, the field of advertising, and media research has made it one of the technologies of power.

The first full codification of strategic messages for attack and defense was compiled by Aristotle in his *Rhetoric* (c. 330 B.C.). In modern times, brilliant expositions of such strategies are presented in the works of Chaim

Perelman[2] and Kenneth Burke.[3] The discussion of strategies given in the remainder of this chapter is by no means exhaustive, but is only included to provide a sense of the richness and density of this lore. Some strategies that were discussed in earlier chapters will not be included. Others will be discussed in greater detail.

Strategy Number One: Manipulating the Context

Every event is measured against its background. Great and small are relative terms. A common house cat is an enormous monster to a mouse. The same cat is an inconsiderable weakling compared to a Siberian tiger. A barn burning is a major event in a tiny rural community; a major fire is quickly forgotten in teeming Tokyo.

Similarly, one can change the persuasiveness of an argument or appeal by expanding or diminishing the context in which a group of listeners think about it. Let us consider expansion first. By doing what Kenneth Burke has called "expanding the circumference,"[4] one may make a small event seem far more critical than it ordinarily appears. In 1983, United States forces invaded the tiny island of Grenada. In gaining support for this military action, President Reagan presented the case not as one in which a great power was overthrowing the government of a tiny nation; rather, Grenada was presented as a link in a much larger and more sinister chain of events. In invading the island, we were actually meeting a major threat by the Cubans and their Soviet allies to destroy the security and freedom of the entire Caribbean and Central American theatre. This is another example of the famous domino theory which magnifies the importance of small nations. For want of the nail, shoe, horse, soldier, battle, war, and, ultimately, nation were lost.

As Kenneth Burke points out, Cicero was very adept at linking smaller events to larger ones. Each event was a synecdoche, a part that stood for a larger whole, a microcosm of the greater macrocosm. This device is well-illustrated in his self-praise after foiling the Catalinarian conspiracy to burn Rome in 62 B.C. Cataline, a ruined aristocrat and rabble-rouser with a huge following, was plotting to burn Rome and massacre its leading citizens, including himself. After having been tipped off about the plot, Cicero appeared in the Senate, where Cataline himself was sitting, and delivered his famous orations against the bold conspirator, beginning, "How long will you abuse our patience, O Cataline?" The senators were so charged with fiery accusation that Cataline fled the city before he could be arrested. After Cicero had captured and tried the other conspirators and saved the city, he wrote to historians asking them to embellish his part in saving Rome to make it appear even more glorious to posterity. He pointed out that, by foiling Cataline, he had actually saved the

Senate, and that, by saving the Senate, he had saved Rome. Furthermore, by saving Rome, he had preserved the Republic, and, by extension, saved all those millions under its sway from Gaul to Egypt. From this larger perspective, he had saved civilization, and, in the act of saving civilization, he had saved the world and thus fulfilled to the utmost the will of Jove, father of all the gods and master of the universe.

A most fanciful use of this expansion was used by a Cornish nationalist in the mid-1970's whose mocking, half-humorous oration parodied that of two former dictators: "Today Cornwall, Tomorrow Wales, Ireland, Brittany, and the Highlands. For the future, the reclamation of Europe!"

Much of the so-called power of television is said to be its power to interpret the meaning of events. Surely, a part of this definition is the determination of the relative importance of any particular event. Events can be increased or diminished in importance by placing them in a much larger perspective (everything seems small when you consider the vast sweep of historical time) or by causally linking them with larger events. An example of this linkage is a media event that occurs once every four years in February—the New Hampshire Primary. New Hampshire is a tiny state with a unrepresentative population. Yet a victory in this contest is often defined as decisive by the media. Even a defeat may be defined as victory. In 1968, Gene McCarthy was seen as a media winner even with a forty-two percent, second-place finish. His unexpectedly strong showing against the incumbent president was a moral victory. Robert Kennedy entered the race, and Lyndon Johnson announced that he would not run.

Early in the coverage of the 1976 Presidential campaign, the phrase media event was coined to signify the magnification of small happenings. The Iowa caucus of January, 1976 became the young campaign's first media event:

> On the night of Iowa's precinct caucuses, as ninety percent of the state's Democrats were preparing to go bowling or settle in front of their television sets and only ten percent to go out and vote, Walter Cronkite raised the question of what the caucus results would finally mean. The answer he got from CBS reporter, Roger Mudd, was typical of an interpretation that dominated much of the event's coverage. "The English that is applied to these results," Mr. Mudd told his anchor man, "is going to be applied to the media and the politicians themselves."[6]

In the words of Joseph Lelyveld, in a primary election, the actual numbers are not important and "real prize" lies " in the headlines."[7]

Examples of this power through expansion and linkage are found throughout social life. In a marriage, the forgetting of small remembrances may be interpreted by one or the other partner as symptomatic of a more pervasive breakdown of the relationship. Ethnic confrontations are so explosive because of the ease with which personal difficulties are expanded to group conflicts. Indeed, in any close-knit group, criticism of a single member is often construed to include the whole. The "all for one and one for all" spirit is rooted in the very nature of group process. Members must protect the worth and validity of their group, and an attack on one is seen as an attack against all. I recall the bitter frustration of a young corporal who tried to convince his battalion commander that he had knocked out a first lieutenant "not as an officer but as a man."

Contraction: The Finite Problem

The power of the finite problem lies in its single-minded, streamlined reductionism. Only the solvable parts of the problem are dealt with; the unsolvable parts are ignored. A problem is dealt with on the level of changing a specific behavior with the minimum use of resources and effort. The finite solution concentrates on eliminating effects of a problem. As far as possible, it bypasses causes, because causes are often unknown and are usually more complex, numerous and hard to deal with than immediate effects.

The method of finite solution is the source of much of our power over the world. Consider the following common situation. A sick child has a fever. We are not sure of the nature of the illness nor the causes of the fever; however, we do know that if we can eliminate the fever or reduce it substantially, the child will be better able to get a good night's sleep, and will not have to battle an exhausting fever. Our penal system is an example of the application of a symptomatic solution. When an enraged criminal terrorizes a small town, looting stores and shooting out windows, we do not typically spend months of clinical therapy and testing to determine the deep-rooted causes of his behavior. We deal directly with his behavior. We remove him from society as we would quarantine a plague victim or isolate a mad dog. Symptomatic solutions are generally more easily and inexpensively applied to a problem than solutions dealing with far-reaching causes which, often, we do not know.

Mechanistic systems deal only in external behavior. If its definitions of punishment and reward can be accepted by its constituents, the system has, in one sense, solved its problems of productivity, social control and motivation. Analogous to the method of the controlled experiment in the laboratory, the strategy of the finite problem is the same kind of deliberate limitation and framing that is the source of much of our power over the physical world. Because it must ignore feelings and attitudes to work efficiently, it is a power which is often purchased very dearly. Since its only claim is instrumental success, it lacks the support of communal sentiment and historic belief. It is the ultimate secularism.

Concentration on a single, instrumental effect extends beyond the laboratory to the economic arena. The single-minded objective of profit-making greatly facilitates cooperation between technology and marketing. Of course, short-term successes have often meant long-term trouble because products exist in a large system, not a linear mono-causal model, but a complex human ecology. Barry Commoner writes compellingly of the unintended effects of various detergent products on the environment. To design instruments to do one operation supremely well is to prevent them from performing others. The histories of Agriculture and Medicine contain many stories of the surprising ways in which every success seems to create a new problem. New hybrids bring new diseases, along with new productivity and unforeseen vulnerability to parasites, fungi, etc. By ignoring long-term effects, we do not eliminate them. They come to pass all the same. Until failures or long-term effects become apparent, the finite solution will be lauded as a success formula and extended over an ever larger range of problems. Unfortunately, in a society of high mobility and rapid change, decision-makers are often gone before the chickens come home to roost.

During the Great Depression, the Roosevelt Administration did not have a unified, coherent plan to combat the causes of the depression. It did not know the causes of the depression, any more than the dozens of wrangling, noisily disagreeing, "expert" economists who vied for its attention. Lacking a definitive consensus and sorely beset by highly visible effects, the administration engaged in a patchwork of symptomatic solutions. Later mythologists gave this frantic *ad hoc* activity an aura of ideological order and programmatic purpose. Its symptomatic solutions did not, in fact, cure the depression (that was the work of World War II); however, they did furnish the government with an enormous mandate to intervene in many formerly private areas of the national life.

The most dramatic manifestations of this power occur in small groups or highly centralized organizations where the leadership is able to deal directly with subordinates and where the demands on the organization are relatively clear and straightforward. Everyone is familiar with leaders who are permitted to define goals very narrowly and are able to ignore the feelings about the process of solving problems in favor of immediate implementation of solutions. A wonderfully humorous version of this style of leadership is found in the old stories of the "Child Prodigy" of Madison Avenue. Arthur Himmelhoch, thirty-two year old child prodigy of Madison Avenue, was New York's Wunderkind of the 1950's, able to solve any problem that arose in any agency. According to one famous story, the youth walked into a large agency where a coffee commercial was being shot, only to find the employees hurling missiles at one another while an actress sobbed distractedly. When Himmelhoch asked about the nature of the problem, he was told that the agency was in the grip of vast conspiracy, that the problem was bigger than all of them, and that the present problem was the culmination of a long string of disasters. Resolutely refusing to deal with their feelings about the problem, young Himmelhoch kept boring to the heart of the matter. He smiled wanly, like a sober man among drunks, and only asked over and over: "But what is the matter? Tell me specifically, what is the matter?"

At first, the only responses were outbursts of rage. The creative Director said that his work was unappreciated, others that the actors were unintelligent, that the operation had long been sabotaged. Himmelhoch continued to press for a specific description of the event. Finally, a cameraman blurted out: "It is that woman! She has a very strange accent. She is unable to pronounce the names of the coffees in the commercials."

Having struck the level of concrete behavior, the prodigy realized that he had also entered the domain of solvable problems. He dismissed the crew, called in the young woman, coached her on the acceptable pronunciations of two brands of coffee, and sent her back. She pronounced the names correctly during the filming of the commercial. In a few minutes, the crew was crying out that he had saved the commercial, the agency, future revenues, and maybe even western civilization.

Accommodation

Short of the annihilation or nearly complete assimilation of a rival group, power struggles are never resolved on the same level as they are fought. Accommodations are temporary "truce zones" in which a balance of power or equilibrium is agreed upon. The struggle does not die; its overt and highly visible character becomes dormant, and it continues on an institutional level.

Because its overt aspects are no longer apparent, one may assume that the conflict is over and that the warring groups have finally transcended their struggle. It is a rude surprise for everyone when some demographic or economic change arrives to upset the critical balance and another period of open conflict erupts.

The premiere example of the destruction of equilibrium is the nation of Lebanon. During the two decades after World War II, Lebanon was often eulogized as a country where Christians and Moslems lived in peace and harmony, a shining example to a world growing ever more pluralistic. Lebanon was a model of a land where two peoples, supposed to be roughly equal in numbers (if not quite in resources and in influence) shared a happy prosperous community. By 1970, it became apparent that the Moslem birthrate had completely outstripped the Christian, permanently altering the demographic balance. A dominant majority had become a minority. The equilibrium was no longer a resolution, but only an earlier latent stage of an ongoing conflict.

The American South is a particularly rich study in power relations. During the period of desegregation, many white Americans looked back to the period of peace between the races—a period which was supposed to have existed between World War I and 1954. As Martin Luther King pointed out, however, that period was a period of negative peace. Then, the great northward migrations and the mechanization of agriculture reached critical mass, and the old Southern verities that had sustained the caste system were gone. During the period of integration after 1955, conflict moved to a far more overt level. After the walls of segregation crumbled, the tribal nature of the struggle began to erode. The clash of groups of individuals united by a common fate was replaced by a clash of individuals merely multiplied by numbers. Conflict between individuals in a myriad of uncertain situations replaced the old norms of collective behavior until a new equilibrium could be found.

Tokenism is a variety of accommodation. It has little immediate instrumental effect, but it is a powerful symbolic force in cultural warfare. The Roosevelt Administration appointed many Catholic and Jewish judges (an act which did very little to change the lives of ordinary Catholics and Jews) and, thus, won the loyalty of millions of voters for the Democratic party. The Government, because of its position as a representative of the general good and of the entire society, has enormous opportunities to win the loyalty of dissident groups. A token gesture is seen as a gesture of special deference. The naming of Geraldine Ferraro as Walter Mondale's running mate in 1984 had no impact on the economic or political status of women (i.e., it was not a tangible or concrete reward), but it had enormous symbolic power. The North, with its tiny proportion of token Afro-American faces in government, education, and the professions was able to maintain an enormous sense of moral authority over the South during the 1950's and 1960's. The willingness to exaggerate these cosmetic differences, by both sides, shows the power of tokenism as a strategy.

Destruction of Legitimacy

Political power does not rest on coercion alone. Despite its near monopoly on the instruments of violence, one need remember that its use of these instruments is bound by a societal code that extends beyond its control. Thus, every political act must find its justification in a prior moral authority, and it might be said that every political act is an exercise in moral authority.

Because government claims to act for the common good, exposure of hidden partisanship destroys its legitimacy. During the civil rights movement of the 1960's, the interpretation of governmental acts as gestures of partisanship, rather than cohesion, weakened the legitimacy of the federal government. References to President Lyndon Johnson as a "cracker president" and various activists as "limousine liberals" were attempts to characterize the government of the United States as a "white government." This partisan accusation turned the government's acts into masks for partisanship. Even Martin Luther King's references to the government's pace of enforcement as "the tranquilizing drug of gradualism" hinted that the motive was stability for the primarily white constituency as opposed to justice for all.

Similarly, former President Carter's 1976 campaign was a curious example of the destruction of governmental legitimacy as a pathway to power. Carter's rhetoric expressed an image of the United States in which the moral authority and the power structure had become detached from each other; alienation was a badge of morality. Moral authority resided in places like the Ebeneezer Baptist Church and among the rural proletariat of New Hampshire and Vermont. Carter promised to heal this gap and to restore legitimacy with "a government as good as its people."

Tribal Piety

Groups that engage in instrumental alliances bond through the pretense that theirs is primarily a moral alliance. The ways in which various political and religious groups "use" each other can be explained in this way. The style and symbolism of Carter encouraged fundamentalist Christian groups throughout his campaign. Once elected, he made it clear, again and again, that he made a strong distinction between his private morality and public policy. Translation: Private values are honored, but not instrumentalized in a secular society, but I am willing to use them to promote symbolic cohesion.

A variety of tribal piety has been called by Kenneth Burke "secular prayer."[8] It is a kind of symbolic compensation. Secular prayer is a commonplace of political rhetoric. If a group must be denigrated, the sharpness of the blow is often softened by a symbolic reward. At the point of attack, the group is elevated. Thus, if corporate taxes must be raised, the announcement of the new policy is couched in terms that praise corporate productivity and the business ethic. When the effect of a policy is to draft men and send them to fight overseas, they are celebrated as if they had been given a high privilege. These gallant young men have been given a special mark of favor and a unique opportunity.

Strategies of Syntax

Strategies of syntax, a term invented by William Bailey, refers to organizational control of individual behavior through a set of abstract rules. Social control by syntax is control-by-rules and by precise measurement. Precise measurement allows the superior in an organization the luxury of making only quantitative judgments. Governance by syntax lends a bogus facade of rationality, fairness, and objectivity to the decision-making process.

Consider the following illustration. In a small college undergoing retrenchment, two young assistant professors, one from English Literature, the other from Biochemistry, are considered for tenure. It is clear that only one tenure track remains because of the prospect of severe long-term retrenchment at the institution. Each scholar has produced a textbook, two teaching manuals and is essentially equal in teaching and service; however, in the area of journal articles, the biochemist has one more published monograph than the literature scholar. The dean, whose background is astronomy, and his tenure committee (with backgrounds in History, Sociology, and Music) are unable to make a qualitative judgment of the actual scholarly merit of the publications of either scholar. After a short deliberation, the dean, with full support of the committee, recommends that tenure be granted to the biochemist. Their reason: he has one more journal article title (they did not descend to counting pages) than the young, English Literature scholar. The process has been expedited by counting. The judgment is unassailable. Quantitative judgments are always easier to make than qualitative judgments, and they are highly persuasive in a culture where bigger is usually better and constant growth is a national imperative.

To decide the quality of each professor's contribution would have required a much more costly and time-consuming process. It would also have required more input by peers. Finally, it would have appeared much more "subjective" and, therefore, open to outside challenge. It may even have been taken as an indicator of the college's values, policies, and long-term goals.

This power tactic is dehumanizing in the sense that it refuses to come to grips with individual experience, imposes a bogus uniformity of products that does not exist, and treats individuals as functions (means rather than ends).

Because of its origins, management has often been seen as a syntactical means of control. It originated in the work of Frederick Taylor,[9] who attempted to increase efficiency and productivity by removing the control of job performance from the workers. From the time of the medieval guilds, workers had been able to control the pace, atmosphere and quality of production. Until late in the nineteenth century, the foreman was seen as a clumsy interloper in the production process; true power over the production process lay with the workers.

Taylor, alive during the time of mass immigration and the relative decline of the power of craft workers, saw his task as one of "massifying" the workers and reducing the level of their skills. Taylor's method of wresting power from the workers was to impose precise rules, instructions and incentives. He broke each job down into its constituent motions and analyzed them to determine which were absolutely essential. He timed the workers with a stop watch to determine the optimum time for each operation. He then eliminated all superfluous motion. The workers followed Taylor's time-patterns with machine-like regularity and greatly increased their productivity. He further recommended a division of labor; for example, some workers were given specialized status as tool maintenance, foremen, etc. Since Taylor's day, despite the continual demands of employers and workers for more education, there have been eras when workers have needed fewer skills and a lower degree of education. Syntactical control, with its demands for routinization, productivity, and efficiency, is more likely to centralize power than to democratize it.

Conclusion

In this chapter, we have begun to touch on the ethical dimensions of power. Insofar as one is confronted with conscious choice in matters of power, one is faced with questions of ethics. The organization of resources always has consequences which can be called good or evil, and, to some extent, those consequences are foreseeable. The last chapter, in particular, will consider the age-old dilemma of western civilization since the Renaissance: how does one give rise to the modern power state without diminishing and denigrating the individual? In many cases, the modern West has substituted coercion for manipulation. In a highly mobilized society, the illusion of free consent must be maintained, and it is often engineered at great cost to the individual. This problem, too, will be discussed later.

Notes

[1] In Plato's dialogue, *Gorgias*, Socrates uses the sophistic concern with "probability" to convince the young Phaedrus of the deeply anti-philosophical nature of rhetoric. In the late twentieth century, the sophists have undergone a rehabilitation from their nadir at the hands of Arnold of Rugby, Jebb, Jowett, and other admirers of the Platonic Socrates. For a far more sympathetic account of a practicing sophist, see John Poulakos, "Gorgias Encomium to Helen and the Defense of Rhetoric," *Rhetorica: A Journal of the History of Rhetoric,* (Autumn 1983), pp. 1-16.

[2] Perelman's work is cited elsewhere here. In one of his last published articles, he brilliantly delineated the reasons for the long eclipse of rhetoric among European intellectuals and its modern rebirth. See Chaim Perelman, "Rhetoric and Politics," *Philosophy and Rhetoric,* 17 (1984), 129.134.

[3] For a brilliant exposition of the creative possibilities of Burke, see Philip M. Keith,

"Burkeian Invention from Pentad to Dialectic," *The Rhetoric Society Quarterly,* (Summer 1979), p. 140.

⁴Ibid. For a fuller theoretical grounding, see Charles W. Kneupper's companion article, "Dramatistic Invention: The Pentad as Heuristic Procedure," *The Rhetoric Society Quarterly*, (Summer 1979), pp. 130-136.

⁵John Carey, "How the Media Shape Campaigns," *Journal of Communication,* 26 (Spring 1976), 50. For a more recent analysis of the relationship of the New Journalism to politics, See Donald L. Eason, "The New Journalism of the Image-World," *Critical Studies in Mass Communication* (March 1984), pp. 51-65.

⁶Joseph Lelyveld, "Press and Politics," *New York Times,* 31 January 1976, Sec. 1, p. 22, col. 1.

⁷Ibid.

⁸Kenneth Burke, *A Grammar of Motives* (New York: Prentice-Hall, 1945), p. 393.

⁹The philosophy of Frederick Winslow Taylor, the founder of scientific management, is described in his *Principles of Scientific Management* (New York: Harper and Bros., 1911; rpt. 1915), as well as in the biography, *Frederick W. Taylor, Father of Scientific Management,* 2 vols. by Frank Barkley Copley (New York: Harper and Bros., 1923).

5

Group Power

Power has two components: mass and unity. Power results from the unification of mass and is achieved through the mobilization of resources.

The power of a particular group is a product of the size of its resources and its potential for unity. A small, highly organized group may dominate a much larger, unorganized mass because the smaller group has been mobilized for decisive, unified action. Similarly, a huge mass of people—despite infinitely greater resources (numbers, wealth, skills, and knowledge)—may be easy prey for a small, elite group because the larger group's members lack a unifying consciousness, singleness of purpose, and an intensity of organization necessary to bring their aggregate bulk to bear. In the Soviet Union or in modern China, the Communist party is an inconsiderable minority; yet, it is able to dominate masses whose potential strength is infinitely greater. In the eighteenth and nineteenth centuries, relatively small but highly mobilized European states subdued enormous tracts of Asia and Africa by discrediting their cultures and smashing their basis of unity. In many civilizations, tiny elites have forced huge underclasses into servitude.

First and last, it should be noted that mobilization is a state of consciousness; it has a grounding in material interests, but the enduring essence of mobilization is spiritual. If the moral ethos of a group remains intact, it can resist the most terrible butcheries and recover from the most thorough dominion. The unifying consciousness of the Greeks and the Jews have allowed these historic peoples to survive as entities, despite the periodic losses of nationality, territory, political sovereignty, and even ethnicity. Stillman and Pfaff have argued that the Arab and the Russian civilizations were not assimilated by the nineteenth century explosion of Western power because they were able to retain their own cultures and their spiritual identities.[1] The great Western model of elite control is itself based upon the organization of moral and intellectual resources. In Plato's great vision, The Republic, the ruling elite had a monopoly on intellectual resources and its capital amounted to a body of organizational skills, received insights, and control over methods of socialization. The means of mobilization are many, but its core is always a shared consciousness.

Dominant groups live in continual fear that some plausible demagog may find a means of temporarily unifying their underlings against them. They can only dominate the masses by facing them as isolated individuals. In the eighteenth century, a partial and temporary mobilization of the masses swept the ruling class from the face of France. After 1945, the colonized Indo-Chinese, Indonesians, and Algerians—demoralized clients of the Western powers during the nineteenth century—gained a unifying national ideology and drove the technically superior, but numerically inferior, whites from their territories.

Whoever has built a constituency is to be feared. Those who have done so have discovered a basis upon which to unify people outside the prevailing power structure. However temporarily, they have forged an alternative consciousness that may serve as a rival means of organization in times of crisis. If an alternative leader's organizing ideology is unassimilable, it may be a dangerous example to others. Thus, in the devolution scare of the late 1970's and early 1980's, it might be argued that the early example of Irish nationalism begot Scot Nationalists, and Scots begot Welsh. If the Welsh had spawned Cornish and Northumbrian Nationalists, the old psychic center, the predominant partner would itself be dismembered.

Two points should be made here. First, much of the literature on power is pathological. It concerns the strength of individuals to force compliance on the part of other individuals.[2] The limitations of this literature are apparent when one recalls that most power is a product of group or institutional arrangements. Secondly, power is often thought of as the ability to terrify and crush subordinates. While such power is temporarily effective, it is inherently unstable and easy to avoid. Further, mass violence is becoming morally repugnant in societies that practiced it freely little more than a generation ago.[3] Even totalitarian regimes now use methods to maintain power that are primarily rhetorical, such as socialization, propaganda, and public demonstration. Truly useful power is an habitual compliance to authority. It is regular, predictable, and institutionalized.

The means by which compliance is justified and extended is the province of the persuader, the practicing rhetorician. Accordingly, the remainder of this chapter will consider the kinds of mobilization, and some particular means of mobilizing groups.

The Kinds of Mobilization

Mass x Unity = Power

Mobilization is of two kinds: episodic and systemic. Episodic mobilization is a temporary unification of people for a limited end. Systemic mobilization is a far more ambitious affair. It is a long-range organization of a constituency for a particular program. The names episodic and systemic do not describe discreet patterns of behavior. They are pervasive human tendencies and are found in a wide variety of cultural settings.

The term episodic mobilization best describes the forensic triumphs of ancient sophists, the marketing strategies of advertising executives, or the campaigns of centrist politicians. It characterizes the passing victories of a dynamic, relatively open, mass society. Short-range and opportunistic, it employs all the traditional forms of persuasion. Ideally, those who engage in episodic mobilization neither attempt to discredit conventional beliefs nor do they try to introduce a new vision of the world. They seek out and employ the beliefs of the masses, current cultural obsessions, and time-honored slogans and shibboleths in buttressing their appeals to get people to vote, to make particular consumer choices, or to support various institutions.

An advertising agency's marketing of a product is a premiere example of episodic mobilization. The advertisers attempt to make their product relevant to fantasies that their customers may already possess about the product, or they try to demonstrate how the product fits into the patterns of their consumers' lives. Thus the backpack and the bicycle are easily marketed, since they allow people to participate in outdoor recreation or to operationalize their ecological consciousness.

Politics is another area of episodic mobilization. In general, American politicians understand that their survival depends upon the execution of adroit and opportunistic mobilizations. A working politician must spend considerable time turning politically indifferent masses into temporary constituencies. The reasons for the primacy of episodic mobilization are rooted in the political culture. First, mass democracy is predicated on the belief that all morally legitimate power resides in the people and must be delegated by them. Second, personal power sought for its own sake is viewed as dangerous and immoral; however, power effectively far greater than that enjoyed by ancient kings and tyrants may be delegated to elected rulers if it is justified as being done on the people's behalf.[4] Thus, rulers of modern democratic states may conscript huge masses of citizenry, confiscate more than one third of the income of their subjects, and appropriate private resources whenever they are licensed to do so by a modest majority. On the other hand, the most formidable majorities dissolve, and entropy attacks the strongest organizations. Majorities are in constant flux; hence, politicians must follow opinion more often than they lead it.

If a dominant majority of voters find a particularly salient issue abhorrent, the most gifted politician cannot oppose them and prevail. A godlike genius could not have stood for racial equality in the South of 1895 and have been elected to the United States Senate. It is doubtful if such a radical would have been perceived as a viable candidate even by the minority who might have given him their silent consent. The same genius probably could not have stood for explicit racial inequality and have triumphed in a single Southern state after 1976. In American politics, numbers are of central importance. Polls, questionnaires, political rallies, and speeches are attempts to organize, to collect, and to intensify support that already exists. Politicians may attempt to crystallize opinion or even misrepresent it, but they are always bound to it, and they can never move far from it.

Indeed, the economic and political systems of the modern West grew up as eighteenth century twins. Both capitalism and democracy are supposedly instruments for the study of the purely formal means of persuasion, proving that the ancient science of rhetoric remains an eminently useful pursuit.

The second kind of mobilization, systemic, attempts a massive, long-term alteration of belief. It not only builds upon experiences and ideas already present within a constituency, it also seeks to define the terms of public reality, to create new opinion, new consciousness, and a new way of perceiving experience. This is the kind of mobilization envisioned by, although never fully realized by, totalitarian movements. The opportunism and revisionism of even the most impeccably totalitarian regimes guarantee a good deal of episodic innovation. On the other hand, there is a strongly systemic impulse in mass movements, religious organizations, indeed, in any complex activity that bids for our allegiance.

In his historic duels with the old sophists, Plato exposed his adversaries as men whose persuasion drew "upon the opinion of the masses rather than truth."[5] He noted that these opinions were undergoing constant change and that the power the sophists derived lasted only until the masses were infatuated by another illusion.[6] In contrast, systemic mobilizers are not content to achieve power through temporary crystallizations of an ever-shifting opinion. Systemic mobilization means the elimination of personal choice by manufacturing opinion—by controlling ideas at their very source. The ancient opportunists were shallow tricksters content with fleeting triumphs at the expense of truth. Modern totalitarians seem content only with a long-range victory through the elimination of choice itself.

Systemic mobilization uses all the formal devices of rhetoric, but it also arrives with its own vision. It has its own definitions and its own channels of dissemination. In its pure form, it differs from episodic mobilization as absolutist ideology differs from opportunistic argumentation.

Although systemic mobilization is an ancient dream, the achievement of a truly systemic mobilization of power has been relatively rare. The great majority of societies, from Greco-Roman times forward, have always allowed an area of personal freedom. Despite the frightful brutality of Nero's court, Seneca could still write about freedom of the will and independence of thought. Under Augustus, Horace could celebrate the virtues of a rich private life. Diogenes could abuse Alexander. Stoic philosophers continued to practice their ideals of personal autonomy during the reign of the twelve Caesars.

Even the most ambitious despotisms have been partial and incomplete. Historically, tyrants have not been interested in the alteration of habitual states of consciousness or of attitudes. For the most part, they have contented themselves with only enforcing certain patterns of behavior. No matter how oppressive the state became, its interest was seldom in controlling the basic content of personal belief. If nothing else, one could always entertain an ideal model of human conduct beyond the reach of the physical and historical world.

Modern ideology, on the other hand, has been greatly amplified and made ubiquitous through centralized mass media, and, thus, makes a closer approach to systemic power. After three generations of propagandizing and early socialization in the Soviet Union, it is no longer necessary to rule by coercion. Like a poisonous spider, totalitarian ideology renders its victim semi-paralytic before it attacks. Its initial vision is not seen as an alternative perspective so much as it is viewed as *The Vision,* and the acting out of its scenario is experienced as historical necessity. The vision becomes a self-fulfilling prophecy, since it is treated as an inevitable outcome of history. It is a guide to conduct because no other courses of action are believed to exist.

The Means of Unity

To ask "What good is power?" is tautological. Power is not a thing, a commodity that may be purchased at a shop. Power is an underlying constant of all human relationships. Human cooperation depends routinely upon group mobilization.

The sources of power in a modern society are mass institutions. These are our military, educational, religious and political arrangements. Obviously, these institutions structure our behavior through many instruments that are not strictly a part of the province of the study of communication. Mass institutions employ force, patronage, high-technology, alliances, external threats, and countless other acts of which communication behavior is only a part. Of course, a major part of institutional mobilization is carried out by means of the communication skills of a tiny part of its membership. The communication skills of the practicing persuader as journalist, advertiser, and politician have long been identified. Only slightly less well-known is the role of ideology in the formation of mass compliance. The next two chapters will deal with the communication skills of the leadership groups and the role of ideology and myth in organizational life.

Notes

Note: Chapter 5 was published in an earlier form as "Power: The Rhetoric of Mobilization," *Central States Speech Journal,* (Fall 1978), pp. 147-154.

[1] Edmund Stillman and William Pfaff, *The Politics of Hysteria* (New York: Harper and Row, 1964), pp. 52-53.

[2] An example of the sort of literature that deals with power as individual influence is Michael Korda's *Power! How to Get It, How to Use It* (New York: Ballantine Books, 1975).

[3] Zbigniew K. Brzezinski, *Ideology and Power in Soviet Politics* (New York: Frederick A. Praeger, 1962), pp. 33-34.

[4] William Campbell, "Political Economy: New, Old and Ancient," *The Intercollegiate Review,* 12 (Winter 1976-77), 68.

[5] Plato, "Phaedrus," *Plato's Dialogues,* Vol. 1, trans. Jowett (New York: Random House, 1937), p. 260.

[6] Plato, "Theaetetus," *Plato's Dialogues,* Vol. 2, trans. Jowett (New York: Random House, 1937), p. 172.

6

The Power of Elites

The Nature of Elites

Why Elites?

It seems that elites, like the poor, are always with us. In all communities, power is shared unevenly. Even in societies where power is widely dispersed, a disproportionate number of crucial decisions are made by a relatively small number of people. Whether they call themselves the servants of the people or their masters, the elite is the ganglion of society. They are the custodians of the community values. They will set the agenda, define the problems, and formulate the solutions. They will enjoy access to the resources of the entire community and the authority to command them. In time of crisis, they will be rushed to the helm. When traditional wisdom fails, innovation will be expected of them. When they fail, the social order may be shaken to its foundations.

The Importance of Elites

The origin, recruitment, education, and competence of ruling groups is of great importance to a community, since the dreams and destiny of every member is in their hands. Thus, where the elite come from, how they are trained, and what their core skills are make up a critical part of the survival formula of every community. Their loyalty to the community and their commitment to its beliefs must be carefully nurtured. On the one hand, consciousness of a kind of superiority may well be necessary for their ability to act with self-confidence and dispatch. On the other hand, too great a sense of separation from ordinary people may turn the elite into a gathering of birds of prey.

One of the core skills of modern elites is the art of persuasion. Most societies maintain at least an illusion of rationality and accountability. Decisions must be undergirded by argument and skillful rhetorical appeal. Much of what elite groups do is talk, among themselves and to others, in a strategically stylized and purposeful way.

Elites in Historical Context

Historically, elites have varied greatly in character, composition, and core skills. The administrative elites of the Roman Empire were recruited largely from the ranks of the hereditary nobility, the great merchants, the banking community, or from the offspring of the senior civil service. Their education for the imperial administration was designed to produce a loyal, competent, and highly dependable ruling class. Accordingly, their education began with the memorization of fables and maxims so that they might be saturated with conventional wisdom. They graduated to the memorization of heroic epic poetry and to the "moral lessons" of Roman History (then a branch of Rhetoric). Their efforts at composition and public speaking followed formulary rules and were based on the imitation of approved models and canonical texts. Finally, they learned the arts of persuasion; in mock court trials, they learned to argue on both sides of an issue with equal facility. The end product was a *Roman*, steeped in the imitation of heroic models, skilled in the arts of insinuation and verbal combat, and possessed of a ready stock of information drawn from the Roman cultural heritage.

This verbal education prepared an administrative elite to rule over diverse ethnic, tribal, and regional groups whose practices and modes of life had to be brought only into a very rough conformity with Roman standards. Like privileged groups throughout history, the Roman elite attempted to pass its advantages on to its children, and some administrative posts became hereditary preserves of great families.

The Middle Ages witnessed the rise of a feudal aristocracy whose core skills were military and organizational. The nobles of the manor house and the castle were primarily organizers of farm work, but ownership of land and the ability to till and defend it was not the sole source of their power. The peasantry's beliefs in the rightness of an earthly station fixed by birth and also in the natural superiority of the warrior blood of the aristocracy were important power sources brought about by social conditioning. The belief in the authority of rank accounts for the extraordinary stability of society during the Age of Faith.

The other medieval elite, the Clergy, often interlocked with the secular authority, particularly at upper levels. This celibate elite preserved the remains of Greco-Roman culture in its monasteries, maintained a vast administrative network, and provided a unifying language (Latin) and perspective (Christianity). The only source of international unity in a fragmented continent, the Church saved the ruined and depopulated cities of the old Roman Empire from complete abandonment. Used as centers for religious administration, the cities survived to enjoy the great urban revivals of commerce and trade in the early Renaissance.

The main sources of religious power were social, psychological, and organizational. They propagated the dominant salvationist world view out of which the consensual reality was shaped and administered the vast structure of European religion. Of course, despite the theoretical separation provided by the doctrine of the two swords, the Church exercised material power through its control of huge tracts of land and resources.

Modern elites of the United States and Western Europe possess skills not really so different from those of ancient elites. They, too, have formidable communication and managerial skills; however, their justifications for holding power are very different from those articulated by earlier elites and reflect the differing ideological climate of the modern era.

Today, it is not superior blood or divine sanction, but merit that is said to legitimate the exercise of power. Authority must be earned; meritocracy has replaced aristocracy. Power generally comes from below and is awarded only for specific situations. It must be seen to be deserved because of brilliant performance, special knowledge, conspicuous ability, or widely recognized service to others. Power is humble, and its voice is either technocratic or akin to that of Horatio Alger in tone and pitch. It has long abandoned the argot of Divine Right.

What Are Elites?

Machiavelli said, "In every republic there are always two parties: one of the people, the other of the nobles." Human hierarchy has always been with us, and dominance and subordination are social facts. The terms elites and masses seem to have been coined during the turmoil of the French Revolution. We have found them useful in talking about revolution and rebellion since that time. The fearfully vivid image of the spontaneous and highly suggestible mob manipulated by the "genius" and his fanatical street ideologues has been a staple of political consciousness from 1790 on. According to this conception, the mob and the genius constantly rediscover their adversaries in every national revolution. There is a renewable series of oppressor-victims to be purged from the community so that the new world can be born. The old nobility, the high bourgeoisie, the technocrats, the military-industrial complex, the jackals of the Establishment, the Masters of the Mass Media all have been identified as targets of social envy and of undeserved privilege.

While these crude images are too simple to be of much aid in the analysis of power, they do highlight an important truth: even if power is exercised by individuals, it is vested in groups, and the mere affirmation of group identity is a necessary prerequisite to power. Power finds a home in groups because they are organized networks. These ready-made structures contain people who share association, understanding, and habits — all potential ingredients of mobilization. Organizations attract power because they already represent power through the sheer fact of being. One need not ask whether a religious, labor, or military organization has power. The question is how much?

The Bases of Power

Although the moral and psychological unity of elites is the crucial factor in their ability to dominate diverse and atomized masses, there are other sources of power. The power of a leadership group is derived from three bases: a material resource base, a psycho-social base, and an organizational or syntactic base.

The Material Base of Power

People who equate wealth with power tend to think of property (including land, machines, resources, and money) as the sole source of power. Certainly, it is an important source, and, in some eras of history, it has been even more important than it is today. In feudal times, land was the primary basis of social stratification. Peasants exchanged surplus crop yields for protection by nobles. Land use and ownership undergirded class relationships and formed the fundamental basis of power. Of course, it was never the only source. Even at its zenith and despite Marx, certain merchants and town dwellers enjoyed independent power at the margins of the feudal social structure. On the other hand, even high spiritual leaders had their power augmented by ownership of buildings, art objects, land, and other resources.

So strong was the connection between property and power at the height of the industrial revolution, that even Karl Marx supposed that the way to end the powerlessness of industrial workers was through the ownership of their tools. The nineteenth century romantic idea of alienation was based on the loss of ownership and of control of the products of one's own labor. Only in the twentieth century did intellectuals begin to believe that communication skills, organization, and technical know-how were greater sources of power than property.

John Kenneth Galbraith[1] points out that so central was property to power in the latter decades of the nineteenth century that wealthy people expected to be granted deference by the middle class and that their opinions were automatically given more weight than those of other groups. The oratory and the popular literature of the so-called Gospel of Great Wealth seems threadbare to us now, but it was celebrated as a kind of higher wisdom in its day. Russell Conwell delivered his famous "Acres of Diamonds" more than six thousand times. Its electrifying message was that anyone could make it in virtually any locality by identifying local needs and supplying them, a sort of generalized version of Booker T. Washington's[2] admonition to "Cast down your bucket where you are." This obvious truism moved the audience to stormy enthusiasm. John D. Rockefeller's speech "American Beauty Rose" was a collection of pseudo-scientific slogans justifying the survival of the richest. It precipitated an orgy of commercial frenzy wherever it was spoken. Andrew Carnegie foretold the coming of the new era of stewardship by great, fatherly captains of industry. His words were treated as inspired prophecy, rather than as commercials for industrialists. All of these former exhalations of superior minds are quaint reminders of an era when property was the badge of sagacity and engendered a nearly automatic deference.

The Psycho-Social Base of Power

Probably the most important source of a group's power is its sense of identity. Dominant groups are bound together by common interests, habits, values, aspirations, interpretations of the past, and agreement on basic decisions. Group identity is made up of common prejudices and shared images of the world and of the group's role in it. In addition, they may share a common language or argot, and distinctive rituals and procedures. Power is fundamentally a psycho-social unity, a "we" feeling. The degree of group power depends upon the homogeniety of common images and the intensity of attachment to consensual beliefs. A group with weak boundaries can only attain power through great size and a massive capacity for assimilation.

An intense psychological unity can overcome weakness of numbers and poverty of resources. The backwardness of the Prussian junker aristocracy was partially overcome by its own narrow single-mindedness. The homogeniety of this group of owners of 700- to 1000-acre farms was due to their fears of displacement in the rapidly industrializing Germany of the late nineteenth and early twentieth centuries. Their potatoes and cabbage were of marginal value (except as a critical resource in time of war), and their ideas were antique survivals of Brandenberg imperialism. Yet, they were an enormously influential group in Otto von Bismarck's opulent and cultured Germany. They were nearly as influential under the Kaiser's reign, at a time when Germany was the most technologically advanced nation on the planet and German thought was coming to dominate the world in philosophy and aesthetics.

For many generations, writers have written about an American ruling class. In 1956, C. Wright Mills,[3] then the leading American writer on the subject of social class, produced a polemical or conspiratorial work called *The Power Elite*, which proved to be one of the very few best-seller sociology books of the twentieth century. The book warns of a dangerous new ruling class — a Frankenstein military-industrial-political directorate served by willing underlings in advertising and mass media. Rapidly hardening into a regime of caste, these people conspired to keep the masses in a permanent consumer status, atomized, confused, and obsessed with creature comforts. The "power elite" even had a special ideology, a self-serving world view that Mills called "crackpot realism." Crackpot realism was only a mask for their true motive: an Orwellian desire for power as an end in itself.

The so-called Eastern Establishment is a ghostly and amorphous entity. A favorite target of former President Richard Nixon, it is an elite that is highly resistant to precise definition. When its members are "named," they prove to be of very diverse origin and ideology. Most conspiratorial writers find it best to treat the Eastern Establishment as a partially clandestine force whose objectives are not fully known and whose "true" membership can only be guessed at. Nominally Anglo-Saxon and vaguely Protestant (no doubt because of strategic assimilation of ethnic challengers), the Establishment's psycho-social unity is explained in a perspective derived from Thomas Hobbes. In Hobbesian fashion, the Establishment is imagined to be motivated by two visions: one is the pageant of conquest, a ruthless desire for unlimited power; the other is that of a profoundly peaceful social order, the gray light of Winchester School's medieval precincts. These potentially conflicting visions are said to find realization in Tory virtue at home protected by swashbuckling cultural imperialism abroad.

One can speculate that the "groupness" of power lends itself to conspiratorial approaches. Virtually all are written by academic researchers and journalists, perennial outsiders whose mission in life is to tell the outsiders what the insiders are up to.

A strong part of the psycho-social unity of an elite lies in the possession of an ideology, a doctrine which justifies the group's existence and disproportionate power in the community and which serves as a guide for its day-to-day practice. It also functions as a key to the interpretation of events and a program for future action. A far more complete discussion of ideology will be undertaken in subsequent chapters. For now, it is sufficient to remind the reader of the centrality of group identity. Even a relatively powerless group represents a potential for future influence.

The Organizational or Syntactic Base of Power

Organizational sources of power are those derived from institutional networks. Institutions themselves are but routinized agreements for solving recurrent problems. At bottom, they are organized collections of knowledge, resources, and procedures sanctioned by mandates of successful outcomes, loyalty, tradition, and other badges of legitimacy. Organizational sources of power include access to media, control of systems of education and socialization, religious organizations, and familial or kinship ties.

In heavily stratified or authoritarian communities, elites may even have control over their own recruitment; they may be able to determine what constitutes knowledge and what constitutes evidence. They may control some of the criteria of success and failure. Two outstanding literary examples are the Philosopher-Kings of Plato's *Republic* and the ministries of Orwell's *1984*. The ruling elites of several communist countries come close to exercising this sort of apparatus power—a power which is nothing less than the ability to define the nature of reality.

The power of organization is vividly demonstrated each time a ruling group is forced to utilize its power. With steely resolution, it presents a united front against disorganized individuals (whose vastly greater numbers make them potentially far more powerful). It is a test of strength between a disciplined army and a mob. In all societies, everything is done to ensure the isolation and aloneness of the rebel. The justice system of every nation illustrates this strategy; the lawbreaker is tried as a social isolate against the communal panoply of the court. Lawbreakers or rebels do not typically argue that they have acted on behalf of a criminal class and that their deviant behavior is an act of esprit de corps in the finest tradition of countervailing power. Elites always keep the odds in their favor by acting in concert against individuals or small combinations.

Power and Authority: The Question of Legitimacy

In the modern era, it is difficult for elites to rule directly. They must be seen as deserving of their advantaged position. Power must be accompanied by legitimacy. Illegitimate rule can only be maintained by constant violence or coercion—the police state. Genuine authority means entitlement. In a modern democratic state, elites must frame an argument for power. They must provide reasons for their acts, using language that the community will find convincing, moral, and reasonable; thus, elites must be seen to deserve their authority for reasons that reflect the mainstream values of the community.

An elite basing its ascendancy on special skills may argue that it alone can perform a critical task for the good of the whole. For instance, because of its special expertise with money, a commercial aristocracy may argue that it deserves special prerogatives, because it alone knows how to create new jobs, expand wealth, and ensure material progress for all. If the commercial elite is convincing, other groups may agitate less for governmental redistribution of the community wealth through increased taxation, regulation, or outright confiscation. In words once attributed to Andrew Carnegie, they will "accept the idea that money should remain with those who know what to do with it." Similarly, a technological elite might argue that it alone has the right to dispose of resources because of the unmitigated benefits of its inventions.

Since an elite is, by definition, a minority, it must constantly guard against counter-organization. As we shall see in the next section, even a poorly organized majority can easily crush a well-disciplined minority. Thus, an elite must do more than look to its own organization; it must avoid clear-cut issues around which a majority can organize. It may have to accommodate some of its positions. Occasionally, it may assimilate leaders or potential leaders of the underclass.

Elites have justified their privileges in many ways. One of the oldest beliefs of European man is the supremacy of royal blood. It has long been a legitimizing belief for aristocracies. In a democratic, technologically oriented society, an elite may rest its privileges on merit or special knowledge. In a religiously based community, one may claim special piety or administrative genius. Since a totally secular society has never existed, elites usually plead at least some combination of practical ability and moral authority.

In the next sections, we shall turn to the dilemma of legitimacy in times of rapid social change.

Notes

[1] For the following discussion of property as a source of power, I am indebted to the insights of John Kenneth Galbraith's, *The Anatomy of Power* (Boston: Houghton Mifflin Co., 1983).

[2] Andrew A. King, "Booker T. Washington and the Rhetoric of Heroic Material-

ism," *Quarterly Journal of Speech,* (October 1974), p. 323.
[3]C. Wright Mills, *The Power Elite* (New York: Oxford University Press, 1956). Of Mills, Donald Martindale wrote: "To estimate the significance of his contentions, it is necessary to realize that of his generation Mills is probably the number one sociologist in America," in *Social Life and Cultural Change* (Princeton: D. Van Nostrand Co., Inc., 1962), p. 478. See also Mills' *The Sociological Imagination* (New York: Oxford University Press, 1959) and his *Causes of World War Three* (New York: Oxford University Press, 1960) for other insights about power.

7

Group Power Strategies

The victor of today may be the vanquished of tomorrow. Today, he may carry all before him; he is seated on the tiger-skins. Tomorrow, he may squat in some nameless cistern. At this moment, his dominance is unquestioned. It seems a law of nature, inevitable. Today, the victor's definitions are everyone's definitions. His symbols of authority are revered even by his victims. His vision of the world appears to be the only realistic vision. Other views of life may be perspectives; his view is reality. Yet, tomorrow, he may be attacked and his symbols of power subverted. Tomorrow, the victor may be displaced.

America is rich in displaced power groups. Elites of destiny quickly become historical curiosities. In a remarkable burst of creativity, the Federalists created many of the basic institutions of the early republic, but, within two decades, they became rigid and fearful. The old Dutch aristocracy on the Hudson, Southern aristocrats, disinherited Yankees in urban New England, and remnants of once powerful, big-city political machines have become old-fashioned stage figures declaiming to us from the scrap heap of history. Yet, all were once powerful groups. Their members were brothers in destiny, with a vision of life that seemed central, inevitable and real to themselves and their subordinates. Looking backward, the only reality seems to have been their inevitable displacement from the center of American life.

If displacement is a fact of existence, so is the desire of groups to hold on to power as long as possible and to pass on their privileges to their children. Class hardens into caste, and physical force is utilized when myth fails. Much theory and ideology has been based on this central social fact. Hegel conceived the whole dialectic of civilization to be based on the egoistic battle of groups.[1] Rejecting rationalistic individualism, Walter Bagehot holds that the struggle between mass stupidity and elite innovation accounts for all social change. The famous criminologist George Vold[2] sees the whole structure of law as the product of shifting ratios of force between warring groups.

The examination of a multiplicity of past and present groups in positions of dominance suggests that these groups have fought off challenges or rationalized their displacement using broadly similar rhetorical strategies.[3] By this point in the book, the reader will have understood that my basic assumption is that dominance and displacement are recurrent situations in the lives of human groups. This chapter will entertain the idea that there are general rhetorical strategies organic to the situation of power maintenance. These strategies are, however, constrained by particular circumstances or challenges, weapons of verbal persuasion in the battle to maintain one's power.

Human situations commonly contain a number of opportunities that can be seized in order to transform the situation. If a group is challenged, it may consider choices of action ranging all the way from absolute domination to utter rejection and abject withdrawal. As certain human situations are resolved again and again, the patterns of choice become visible. Both successful and disastrous attempts can be named and analyzed.[4] They become self-conscious, streamlined, abstracted, and stylized. These symbolically expressed patterns of action are what we call rhetorical strategies. They are the coping mechanisms, the potential war material of a given situation.

This chapter will describe two sorts of strategies. The first five strategies will be those of groups which are still actively fighting. The last three will be those employed by groups who have been dislodged from positions of power, but are still tormented by the hope of revenge or not fully resigned to their new status as underlings.

Ridicule: Humor as Counterrevolution

Newly emergent groups are highly visible. They are extremely self-conscious in their actions and highly vulnerable. To people who wish them well, their awkwardness is very touching, and the care with which they exercise their new responsibilities is moving. The "humorous" attack on the Women's Suffrage Movement of the nineteenth century is particularly full of examples of this strategy:

> How...funny it would be if Lucy Stone, pleading a cause, took sudden-
> ly ill in the pains of parturition, and gave birth to a fine, bouncing boy
> in court. It would be even more comical if the Rev. Antoinette Brown
> were arrested in the middle of her sermon in the pulpit from the same
> cause. Funniest of all to contemplate, however, concerned Dr. Harriot
> K. Hunt, the female physician, who might, while attending a gentleman
> patient for fistula in ano, find it necessary herself to send for a doctor
> and to be delivered, there and then, of a man or a woman child, perhaps
> twins.[5]

Such humor has several functions. It is hoped that sarcasm will undermine
the self-confidence of the challenger; it will strengthen the club spirit of the
old group by flattering its weakened sense of superiority. It will cause third
parties outside either group to see the emergent group as an aggregation of
social clowns. What is not seen as worthy of serious attack is perhaps not
worthy of serious examination. Finally, the sensitivity of emerging groups
being proverbial, it may be hoped that the sarcasm will evoke intemperate,
rash, and profane replies that can be dismissed as hysterical. Ridicule is, as
Hugh Duncan observes, a weapon that strikes against an opponent's very
sense of identity.[6] The cruel epithet "Afro-Engineering," currently used in
the South and Southwestern United States to denote any piece of
particularly shoddy improvization, is an example of savage ridicule
employed by insecure whites to undermine the new and hard-won identity
of blacks. It reinforces the belief that all genuine technology is so-called
white European technology. The same mind set dismisses the Japanese
achievement by calling its makers "social insects." Kissinger's amazing
statement that nothing south of the Pyrennes was significant is not too far
from Colonel Blimp's frequent remark that "civilization begins north of the
Loire. Below is Wog Land."

Crying Anarchy

When students and workers challenged DeGaulle during the French riots
of 1968, he appealed for unity on the basis of national survival. He framed
the choice for his constituents: the triumph of communism or the survival
of France. Students and workers threatened more than the Fifth Republic,
more than the middle class, more than France's historic universities or
industrial health. "France, indeed, is threatened by a dictatorship...
totalitarian communism."[7] Able to make his case to a nation that had
already permitted him a monopoly of the means of communication, he was
once again to define the choice as DeGaulle vs. Chaos.[8] Most people have a
stake in the existing order of things, and, whenever one's way of life and
material substance are threatened, there is an immediate loss of objectivity.
To cry anarchy is to do more than to brand the activities of the challengers

as merely criminal and sinister. As destroyers of society, they strike at everyone. They are downright devilish.

In the days of the early American republic, the ruling Federalists fought off the new Democratic-Republicans of Thomas Jefferson by raising the spectre of anarchy. As one of their chiefs, Fisher Ames, observed, "The weather is mild since Jefferson was elected; but it is an unwholesome and treacherous softness that seizes the windpipe like an assassin."[9] They warned that the new democracy would destroy a society in which "Providence hath wisely ordained a chain of grades and subordinances from peasant to peer."[10] Aristocrats and merchant princes in a democratizing nation, the Federalists came to see the central theme of history as a struggle between an able and unselfish gentry and a clutch of jealous demagogs who inflamed the spectre of anarchy in defense of their beleaguered elite: "There is a constant tendency in the poor to covet...in the indolent and profligate to cast the burden of society upon the industrious and virtuous; and there is a tendency in ambitious and wicked men to inflame those combustible materials."[11]

The Federalists felt that the siren promises of the Jeffersonians must be resisted at all costs. The Jeffersonian cant about freedom was particularly dangerous, for "the more free the citizens, the bolder and more profligate would be their demagogs."[12] For Fisher Ames, democracy was "like death" and was "only the dismal passport to a more dismal hereafter."[13]

Not long after the decline and fall of the Federalists, Lyman Beecher raised the spectre of moral anarchy, a threatened social order, and a decline of standards. The New Unitarians were reducing the old Puritan army of the faithful to a few hardy remnants:

> It requires no proof, but universal observation to support the position that the irreligious, immoral and voluptuous part of the community prefer the liberal system, and are vehement in their opposition to the evangelical system. If this assertion needs confirmation assemble the pleasure-loving and licentious community of the world, the patrons of the balls and theatres and masquerades, and let the doctrines of the evangelical system be preached plainly to them. Would they be pleased with them? Would they endure them?[14]

During the 1970's and early 1980's, the push for equal employment in formerly all male areas was equally instructive. It produced a defensive rhetoric freighted with images of intellectual chaos and debauched standards. *Time Magazine* notes that, in 1974, ninety-five percent of all full professorships were still held by white males and lamented the unseemly haste with which affirmative action was being pressed in the traditionally all-male (with the exception of Cornell) Ivy League. *Time* dismisses affirmative action quotes as having "accomplished little for minority groups while doing violence to a long tradition of academic independence and excellence."[15] Following a lengthy discussion of feminine aspiration,

Steven Goldberg warns that "women who deny their own nature" are in a position of being "forever condemned to argue against their own juices" and to produce acts that are "terribly self-destructive."[16] Likewise, much of the old segregationist rhetoric promised a long night of barbarism if black citizens were allowed to use public drinking fountains. Twenty years after integration was begun and finally accomplished in his county, a southern relative mused, "I guess it was like most things in life. The actual experience wasn't nearly as terrifying as the anticipation." His anticipation had been set by the horrendous rhetoric that had warned of racial cataclysm.

A defender of the old British Public School, Desmond Hawtrey, in "The Decline of English Education" writes of the Labour government's attempt to undermine Charterhouse, Eton, Rugby, Harrow, and other bastions of privilege.[17] For Hawtrey, the new egalitarianism has produced the modern student whose "admiration for the police state is boundless."[18] Further, the democratization resulting from the Bevan and Butler Act has not only ruined Tory excellence, but has spawned university students whose "violent and intolerant behavior closely resembles the Chinese Red Guards inasmuch as they have the same objects in mind for destruction: old ideas, old culture, old customs and old habits."[19]

The luxury of historical perspective allows modern scholars to judge the dire warnings of former establishmentarians. Generally, they seemed to have indulged in a rhetoric of overreaction. To the establishmentarians themselves or to the third parties faced by the uncertainties of rapid change, the cries of anarchy may often have seemed compelling. Occasionally, they were correct in the long run. During the 1950's, it was considered amusing to recall the dire predictions of the champions of the horse. It was richly comic to think that anti-horseless carriage people once thought that the gasomobile would poison the atmosphere, cause congestion on the roads, kill large numbers of people, destroy the central cities, and create urban sprawl. How clearly they saw the future after all!

Setting Impossible Standards

It is an old truism that whoever is able to define the terms of a conflict situation wins. We go by the "King's English," which overarches the argot of all subgroups. A common application of this is controlling the rules of a game in a way that shuts out interlopers. Old families may use the fact of their antiquity as a badge of prestige. If colonial ancestors are important for membership in an elite, then new immigrants need not apply. All interlopers are by definition new, and it is possible to use tradition as a weapon against them. Much of the literary mythology of New England rural life and the charming sketches of granite Yankee character were developed by poets like Whittier and Longfellow at a time when the old Yankee stock was fighting for its economic and political life in Boston and Providence against the new waves of Roman Catholic immigrants. The attractive New England native framed by Whittier and Longfellow, and later refined by Marquand and Frost, was an exclusive character. In describing ancestral New England to Californians, Detroiters, and Delamarvians, they did their best to pretend that the recent arrivals hardly existed.

Boundaries must keep people inside the group as well as they block others out. Threatened groups are very careful about definitions, for compromise must be resisted, particularly by the members of one's own group. Walter Bagehot correctly perceives the dynamics of this strategy:

> "Whoever speaks two languages is a rascal," says the saying, and it rightly represents the feeling of primitive communities when the sudden impact of new thoughts and new examples breaks down the compact despotism of a single consecrated code.... The old oligarchies wanted to keep their type perfect, and for that end they were right not to allow foreigners to touch it.[20]

The sense of uniqueness, of elitism, of separateness fosters prejudice, the classic defense mechanism against displacement.

Control of others through the mastery of definition is an ancient strategy. God gave Adam and Eve dominion over the Earth by giving them the right to name the beasts of Eden. Socrates dominated his opponents from the very instant they agreed to accept his definitions. Stokely Carmichael believes that the power to define was the key to the dynamics of the master-slave relationship. Black Power was itself a process of rejecting old definitions and making new ones:

> And the power to define is the most important power we have. He is master who can define. That was made clear in the McCarthy period. If McCarthy said you were a communist, you had to get up and say, "No, I am not a communist." He had the power to define. It is the same thing. My fellow Americans, the Communists, the slanted-eyed Viet Cong are our enemy. You must go kill them. You don't have the right to define whether or not that cat is your enemy. The master has defined it for you. And when he says, "Jump," you say, "How high, boss?" So then we must begin to define our own terms and certainly our own concept of ourselves and let those who are not capable of following us fall by the wayside.[21]

To define categories as male or female; jobs as blue or white collar, fulfilling or deadening, high-tech or low-tech; music as black or white; ideas as socialist or capitalist; literature as elite or popular may influence our responses to the world powerfully. People are eager to affirm their identities. One still meets youths eager to blunt their sensibilities on exhausting and brutalizing jobs, because such jobs are said to be manly. Truly the maker of a definition is more like a god than a human being.

Co-optation

The notion of separation is temporary and an illusion. Over the long haul, it may be necessary to adopt the old Johnson's Wax slogan: "Save the surface and you save all." When pressure becomes overwhelming, it may still be possible to assimilate one's rivals. Conventional wisdom holds that it is dangerous to quarantine one's rivals for long periods of time. Enforced isolation makes them utopian and, as Bismarck and the Czar of all the Russias discovered, utopian rivals are the most dangerous rivals of all. Minorities know that institutionalization of their problems brings mixed blessings. Government programs usually bring only half a loaf, and, however inadequate, they destroy the urgency of minority appeals. The classic formula for removing a problem from the arena of public discussion has been the institution of a social program. Leaders of emergent groups sometimes complain that cooperation with dominant groups may be unequal and even dangerous to boot:

> In the United States, as in Africa, their "adaptation" operated to deprive the black community of its potential skills and brain power. All too frequently, these "integrated" people are used to blunt the true feelings and goals of the black masses. They are picked as "Negro leaders," and the white power structure proceeds to talk to and deal only with them. Needless to say, no fruitful meaningful dialog can take place under such circumstances.[22]

In the mouth of a dominant group member, co-optation is presented as the only realistic alternative. It sounds the tone of reason and sweet good sense. Thus, a prominent historian views co-optation as the only reasonable course for third world nations: "The Third World has no option but to risk the synthesis: the blind, reactionary course—the zealot picture of the external world is always defeated."[23] The goal of co-optation is a rather painless assimilation or at least a blunting of competition. The ideal is to achieve a stable equilibrium that is still unequal and still tilted in favor of the dominant group.

Joining the Opposition

Every British and Anglo-American school child once recalled the intrigues of William of Normandy's Senechal in the times before the Conquest of 1066. Bound to William utterly, Senechal pretended to oppose him in the council of barons. Rallying behind him as their champion, the barons made him their spokesman. They were filled with horror when he supinely supported each of the Duke's demands for ships, money, and men.

Golden Age Strategy: The Myth of Consolation

Even in defeat, old elites can contrive to gain an aesthetic victory. They may tell the story of the agony of their defeat in the poetically tragic way that makes it sound like triumph. It is the "let nothing so become us as the manner of our leaving" device used by Churchill to make the ignominious British withdrawal from Empire look like a great humane achievement.

The most innocent example is that of the aged professor laughing with delight over the news of eighteen years of declining SAT scores. It buttresses a favorite academic myth, that of decline from a Golden Age. This golden age nearly always coincides with the youth, or at least the early teaching career, of the professor. During this time, an elite core of highly dedicated students, inflamed with a fierce love of learning, carried out their assignments with imagination and rigor.

More serious was the romantic myth of Southern failure, a fantasy revenge against Yankees. According to this script, the very qualities that allowed Yankees to win the War Between the States condemned most Northerners to wallow forever in coarseness and shallow materialism. Even so brilliant a writer as Richard Weaver purveyed the myth of the greater sensitivity and the higher spirituality of the South.[24] So successful was the Southern myth of consolation, that many Northerners embraced it.

It is easy for outsiders to ridicule myths of consolation; it is not so easy for those whose sense of worth, social role, and image of the world is anchored in a group that is being stripped of its power. If a defeated group is to carry on, it must save face. The consolation myth confers morale on the defeated and makes the fruits of victory turn to ashes in the interloper's mouth. The myth of British cultural superiority and gross American materialism is particularly effective as a piece of fantasy revenge that allows former masters to become resigned to their lot. A so-called special relationship was envisioned by Britishers after World War II to operate in a way analogous to Greek tutors forming the minds of the young Roman Imperials. Thus, American Power would be tempered and directed by European wisdom and experience. Unfortunately, the model worked no better in 1948 than at the time of Polybius. Modern language departments that once displaced the dominant classical studies a little more than a century ago now suffer the same displacement from the Sciences and Social Sciences. They have attacked the displacers with nearly the same arguments that were formerly used against them.

The Official Betrayal Alibi

A related device is the excuse of betrayal. Being a live dog or a dead lion are not the only alternatives in a struggle, the preacher to the contrary. It is flattering to believe that one's group has been undermined by formidable enemies or sold out by one's own people. During the 1950's, many whites eagerly embraced the belief that the new militant black organizations were not organized by blacks themselves, but were being led by white dissidents. John Randolph warned that his beloved Virginia was being destroyed by its own children as they crossed the mountains. He denounced the settling of the West as a "suicidal deed" and called Virginians "the only people so overwise as to acquire provinces not that we might govern them but that they might give law unto us."[25] Randolph prepared his alibi for Virginia's future decadence. Virginians were so gifted that even their destruction came about through an excess of their own creative energy. Henry Adams saw America undermined by the members of his own class. Surely no one else but brahmins could have done it. Tightly knit political groups have always enjoyed betrayals on the ground that only their own members were brilliant enough to destroy them.

The placing of blame is a genteel form of the ancient sacrifice. Resentment must be "diverted" outside the group, just as the ancient priest, "the divertor of the course of resentment" had to get "rid of this blasting stuff in such a way" that it did not "blow up the herd and the herdsman." This was his "real feat" and "supreme utility."[26]

When things go wrong for a group, a nation, or a people, it can be a dangerous time for people on the periphery. The group must reaffirm its integrity, expiate its guilt, and return to its mythical purity. It rarely does so by sacrificing the central or core members. France finds its Dreyfuss, Germany its unassimilated elements, newly emergent African nations their "Asian" merchants. Every group has its devils waiting in the wings. Western states used to find their devils in eastern developers, but the devil switched locations during the 1960's and 1970's. Today, one hears of Southern California developers smashing the ecology, leveling the mountains, and wasting the water of unborn generations for absurdly wasteful lake communities in the heart of the desert. In Eastern New Mexico, wealthy Texans are sometimes seen as devils; in rural Vermont, New Hampshire, and Maine, a convenient devil in the Yuppie. The Connecticut Yuppie is felt to be a promiscuous cosmopolite who exploits the form of New England civilization while crushing the substance. Yuppie ski resorts and cutsey shops raise taxes to unbelievable levels, smashing the remaining farmsteads of the former Yankee Land.

Rebirth or Revenge

An ignominious fall, a humiliating present, and an apparently gloomy tomorrow can be endured cheerfully if only the final outcome is right. Despite flood, earthquake, famine, and reversal of fortune, our little clutch of falcons will return to the heights. The old legends are replete with the promises of dead kings returning to restore their people to greatness. King Arthur will come again and the sleeping Celts reawaken; the South will rise again. Abyssinia will spread its powerful sable wings, and the disinherited rural proletariat will reclaim rural America as Osiris and the vegetation gods return. It happens often enough for hope to sustain those in exile.

The notion of the return is suggested in all of human experience. Nature presents a cyclical pattern. Moon and tides wax and wane. The seasons, the heavens, and the generations revolve endlessly. Religion affirms that one must taste physical death to attain the victory of spiritual rebirth. Dying to self, one gains all the gifts of the gods. For the group whose battle days are past, there will be another chance.

The Ghost Dance religion of the western Dakotas was a systematic attempt to enact this pattern of life, death, and triumphant rebirth.[27] Driven by an unbearably painful sense of displacement, the Indians danced to openly communicate with the dead and accelerate the decay of the cosmic cycle. The cycle's end would mean Armageddon for the European invaders, and a new life for the aboriginal inhabitants of the Plains. The enactment of the drama suggested a public version of the white man's own Faust legend, the renewal of youth.

Against a milder threat, genteel New Englanders turned to Utopian reform to resolve the sense of being nudged aside by the new commercial and industrial aristocracy. The element of competition, the very badge of the new merchant warrior, was systematically extirpated from Brook Farm and a number of other nineteenth century Utopias.

If the older elite can maintain cultural supremacy, it can deny the new elite legitimacy. Long after it has lost power, a group may still hang on to a kind of symbolic supremacy fighting for the maintenance of legal norms and resisting changes in local customs. This accounts for the struggle over the recognition of gambling in Boston as William F. Whyte's brilliant "Street Corner Society" illustrates:

> The policeman is subject to sharply conflicting pressures. On the one side are the "good people" of Eastern City, who have written their moral judgments into law and demand through their newspapers that the law be enforced. On the other side are the people of Cornerville, who have different standards and have built up an organization whose perpetuation depends upon the freedom to violate the law.[28]

And, indeed, as upper-class Boston lost one battle after another with former immigrant groups, it was perceived to have lost cultural power, as well as economic and political power. Losing the power to define cultural and legal norms, Boston itself came to be seen in a new way—by the late 1930's, it could never be thought of again as an Anglo-Saxon Protestant, middle-class city. The battle for symbolic dominance shifted from the public to the private arena. With the changes in Harvard and private clubs, even that arena was given up in the 1960's. Only a repudiation of pluralism could return the old elite to a strong public position—this time as a referee between warring groups.

The fascination of literary intellectuals with a mythical America of lantern slides and clean air is a symptom of the grimness and paranoia that so many Europeans notice just beneath the surface of fun-loving Americans. Novelists and critics of the printed word have suffered a psychological displacement from the cultural center dominated by the newer media of films, radio, and television. Signs of this alienation have long been apparent. On the other hand, the novel was considered a cheap and trashy medium in its day, and now, in its relative eclipse, has reached mountain tops of respectability. During the 1970's, members of the old literary culture wrote endlessly about the decline of style and the new barbarism. It was not surprising that many of their targets were movie stars, athletes, rock stars, and television show hosts. The violent interchanges between Snow and Leavis over the relevance and value of science versus the humanities was long ago identified by Lionel Trilling as a bitter class warfare.[29] Within the modern university, both groups tended to behave as rival clubs battling over issues of prestige and power. Of course, in the 1980's, both groups have been eclipsed by the supine response of university administrations to the vague vocationalism of its majority constituency. Once again, it is well to remember that the new ascendency of the business colleges rests on the same mandate: the practical claims of students.

Conclusion

Conflict is an integral part of the experience of dominance. New clusters of power are always arising to challenge the old. Since continuous, direct combat is physically and emotionally exhausting, schemes of limited warfare have been worked out. The eight group strategies discussed here are examples of limited warfare. Their very constraint cuts losses, minimizes risks, and avoids the social instability that accompanies crushing defeat. Combat needs rules, and its arts can become codified as objects of study.

It is instructive to think of the rhetorical strategies discussed here in terms of a wrestler's repertoire of holds. The first five are catches and holds designed for victory. They do not fall into any natural sequence or hierarchical arrangement. The situations for which they are apt are like the opportunities in a match when one's opponent is easily throttled and hurled to the mat. The last three are largely defensive. With them, one hopes for a graceful loss or the option to return and fight another day. The fighter who cannot roar hoarse triumph can still hang on to some shreds of power and regroup for the future.

The strategies are the gladiator's blueprint for victory. The employment of a particular strategy depends upon time, chance, and the appearance of a special weakness, for the weaponry of rhetoric is situational. Thus, like the old Greek heroes whose struggles seemed grandly stylized, the struggles of modern power groups are paradigmatic, patterned, strategic—driven by the desire for dominance.

Notes

General Note: This chapter is a revision of an article originally published as "The Rhetoric of Power Mobilization: Elites at the Precipice," *Quarterly Journal of Speech,* (April 1976), pp. 124-137.

[1] Hegel felt that civil society rests on two foundations: that individuals aim only at their private interest and that individual interests are so related that the satisfaction of one depends on the satisfaction of others. For the clearest exposition of Hegel's notion of society as a competition of egos, see his *The Philosophy of Right,* tr. S. W. Dyde (London: George Bell, 1890), Sec. 185.

[2] The last major American conflict theorist was George Bryan Vold, a criminologist who retired from active work in 1962. In America, the School is expiring from lack of followers, rather than from theoretical weaknesses. It has a long and distinguished European history. The fullest interpretation of the role of conflict in human institutions was advanced by Polybius, the son of a statesman of the Achaean League, in *Histories,* 2 (c. 205-125 B.C.): pp. 37-40, p. 43; and 6: pp. 11-18. The Epicurean school was strongly shaped by his doctrines and so were those of Lucretius, Horace, and Livy. For a recent analysis, see Kurt von Fritz, *The Theory of the Mixed Constitution in Antiquity: A Critical Analysis of Polybius' Political Ideas* (New York: Columbia University Press, 1954). After the Roman world fell, theologians found conflict theory inconsistent with their ideas, but the theory continued to receive expression in the Arab world, especially through the Tunisian, Ibn Khaldun. The best sources of Ibn Khaldun's ideas are Duncan B. MacDonald, ed., *A Selection from the Prolegomena of Ibn Khaldun* (Leiden: E.J. Brill, 1905), and Mushin Mahdi, *Ibn Khaldun's Philosophy of History* (London: Allen and Unwin, 1957). Famous theorists of modern times are Machiavelli, Jean Bodin, Thomas Hobbes, David Hume, Adam Ferguson, Adam Smith, Thomas Malthus, Karl Marx, Herbert Spencer, William Graham Sumner, Walter Bagehot, Gustave Ratzenhofer, and Albion Small. The nearest approach to conflict theory today is found in the works of Peter Berger and Thomas Luckman. See especially their *The Social Construction of Reality* (Garden City, New York: Doubleday Anchor Book, 1967). They focus on the notion of society as subjective reality. In their view, society is not transcendent—humans create their own social reality and then "see" it as objective, an entity independent of man, existing over, and beyond, him. The ideological bias of this approach is readily apparent, for its existentialist grounding maximizes both human freedom and man's moral duty to make both himself and society. A modified conflict position may be found in the work of Thomas Szasz. See especially his *Ideology and Insanity* (Garden City, New York: Doubleday, Anchor Book, 1970).

[3]Some conflict theorists have never been more than a short step from ideology (a set of ideas to justify practice), while more than a few have featured overt social programs aimed at an ultimate goal of social stability. Very often, these thinkers have found in the vindication of almost any action a goal of achieved order. For example, Machiavelli's prince achieved stability through cunning actions designed to preserve an equilibrium of forces within the state. For Polybius, legitimate power was that power which could be made to "appear" stable, however arbitrarily it actually operated. Sorel wished to bludgeon his own society to death in order to achieve a powerful technology whose free play would no longer be stultified by human passion and human sentiment. Vilfredo Pareto guaranteed an equilibrium of forces through the circulation of elites. Livy saw Roman Imperialism as an outward manifestation of the heaven-directed conflict that would bring to all the gift of peace. Contemporary theorists such as Joseph Gusfield [see his *Symbolic Crusade* (University of Illinois-Urbana Press, 1963)] have stressed the notion of cultural victory in their studies of status politics, while Kenneth Burke has given much attention to guilt and purgation as important features of group struggle.

[4]Lloyd F. Bitzer, "The Rhetorical Situation," *Philosophy and Rhetoric,* I (1968), 1-14, develops the concept that rhetoric is situational.

[5]Stewart H. Holbrook, *Dreamers of the American Dream* (Garden City, New York: Doubleday, 1957), p. 185

[6]Hugh Dalziel Duncan, *Communication and Social Order* (New York: Bedminster Press, 1962), pp. 404-405.

[7]Brian Crozier, *DeGaulle* (New York: Charles Scribner & Sons, 1973), p. 635.

[8]Ibid.

[9]Fisher Ames, *Works,* I, rev. ed. (Boston: Little Brown, 1954), p. 256.

[10]From John C. Miller, *The Federalist Era, 1789-1801* (New York: Harper & Row, 1963), p. 118.

[11]Ibid., p. 112.

[12]Ibid., p. 113

[13]Ibid.

[14]Ernest Wrage and Barnet Baskerville, *American Forum: Speeches On Historic Issues, 1783-1900* (Seattle: University of Washington Press, 1960), p. 103.

[15]"Affirmative Action: The Negative Side," *Time,* 15 July 1974, p. 86.

[16]Steven Goldberg, *The Inevitability of Patriarchy* (New York: Morrow, 1973), p. 229.

[17]Denis Hawtrey, "The Decline of English Education," *The Intercollegiate Review,* 8 (1973), 117-122.

[18]Ibid., 122.

[19]Ibid.

[20]Walter Bagehot, *Physics and Politics* (New York: Knopf, 1948), p. 42.

[21]Stokely Carmichael, "Speech at Morgan State College," *The Rhetoric of the Civil-Rights Movement,* ed. Haig Bosmajian and Hamida Bosmajian (New York: Random House, 1969), p. 115.

[22]Stokeley Carmichael and Charles V. Hamilton, *Black Power* (New York: Random House, 1967), p. 31.

[23]Edmund Stillman and William Pfaff, *The Politics of Hysteria* (New York: Harper Colophon, 1964), p. 188.

[24]See Richard Weaver in *Southern Renascence: The Literature of the Modern South,* ed. Louis D. Rubin, Jr. and Robert D. Jacobs (Baltimore: Johns Hopkins Press, 1953).

[25]Russell Kirk, *John Randolph of Roanoke: A Study in American Politics* (Chicago: Regnery, 1964), p. 39.

[26]Friedrich Nietzsche, "The Principle of Resentment," in *Sociology and Religion,* ed. Norman Birnbaum and Gertrud Lenzer (Englewood Cliffs, New Jersey: Prentice-Hall, 1969), p. 105.

[27]See Robert M. Utley, *The Last Days of the Sioux Nation* (New Haven: Yale University Press, 1963). Accounts of the dances are contained in Chapter Six.

[28]William F. Whyte, *Street Corner Society,* 2nd ed. (Chicago: University of Chicago Press, 1955), p. 138.

[29]Lionel Trilling, *Beyond Culture: Essays on Literature and Learning,* (New York: Viking Press, 1968), pp. 145-177.

8

The Communication of Power in the Popular Arts

Art as an Environment

In his journey to the Hebrides, Boswell tells how he and Dr. Johnson came to a storm-swept, desolate promontory. Here they found superb accommodation in an army blockhouse. With a great fire, excellent wines, a crown of lamb garnished with rude spices, brilliant company, unexpectedly rich furnishings, and magnificent service, it amused Boswell to gaze out over the dark, barren wastes where the wind and rain were raging audibly. He and Johnson found it a matchless example of the "wonder and power of human art." The wonder and power of human art have advanced considerably since Boswell's famous tour. The miracle of air conditioning has produced Houston and Phoenix, and European man has penetrated to every corner of the globe, isolated from his true environment by a world of comfortable artifice.

The aesthetically mediated world of the late twentieth century is heavily mortgaged in its future and psychologically alienated from its past. Its apparent triumph is so complete that we forget how recent it is. The little village of my childhood (now utterly transformed by developers and thousands of "seekers" who smashed the old social system) was girdled by woods on one edge and by hundreds of acres of cornfields on the other.

Those who lived on the outlying farms were at the mercy of sun, wind, rain, hail, and early frost. Bird flights, the appearance of corn silk, the behavior of animals were taken as important signs by more than a few.

In adulthood, I came to live in cities. Here, I came to know an almost totally human environment, the peoplescape of the urban wilderness. The signs of this environment were constructed by human beings. They were, for the most part, deliberate, self-conscious, and intentional. One's knowledge of the urban environment is mediated through these signs. Reality is mediated; it is a reality of artistic symbols.

Accordingly, one's mode of gaining knowledge about the world is different. In the country, one estimated the size of the harvest by looking at it. Standing first at the border of the wheat field and then stepping into it, a practiced eye could tell whether it would yield thirty or forty or fifty bushels of wheat. Today, I may look at statistical tables, listen to reports from the Department of Agriculture, or talk to a speculator at the corn exchange. Like almost everyone else in North America, my picture of reality is derived from paper or electronic signals. This is a reality taken on faith; it is beyond my immediate experience, and I interpret it according to its consistency with the messages I have received in the past from the public media.

Further, many of my most important guides to behavior do not arise from the crucible of face-to-face human interaction. These come from books I have read, plays, news broadcasts, and, perhaps, even from advertisements. My estimate of politics is powerfully influenced by the public media who select, and therefore set, the public agenda of significant issues. Indeed, it has become the accepted role of the public media to determine the relevance and importance of events, to interpret their meaning, and to arrange them within an aesthetically satisfying form — usually a narrative.

It is instructive to ask a late-twentieth century person, "How do you know the things you know?" Despite the so-called scientific character of the times, the individual thus asked will seldom produce empirical proof. Instead, he or she will offer an abstract, a dictionary, a printout, an authoritative report, a popular magazine article, a synopsis of "expert" hearsay, or even an editorial. Will we expect better results with our leadership class? Perhaps they draw upon a fund of direct experience, but most of their working data comes from index cards, reports, video screens, files, and books. Reality is paper.

What we learn about the world is largely determined by the power arrangements and economic opportunities in our national communities. Our "news" is influenced by sound marketing principles. A story of finding two young American skiers in the Alps is judged to be of more interest than that of two hundred people stranded in the snows of Nepal. We can predict that there will be more news about the rich and famous than about the poor and lonely. When stories about the poor appear, they will generally be labelled "human interest."

Popular Art as an Expression of Power Syntax

The struggle for power is the subject of much attention. Religious sermons are filled with images of heavenly power and of the war between the forces of Good and Evil. Conflict is a recurrent theme of art. The theme of dominance is chronicled in painting, advertisements, novels, theatre productions, movies, and popular music. Further, popular art uses the language of power, a language recognizable to the audience, since it is expressed in its conventional communal symbols. This language of power is sometimes obtrusively enacted in the foreground of a work of art. At other times, it is the background or underlying syntax of the art form. Plays, novels, and films contain messages of deference for some groups and messages of denigration for others. Popular art both reflects and reinforces our beliefs about power in society. Because art is everywhere, its very matter-of-factness causes us to accept its meanings as a matter of course, and, thus, to underestimate its influence. Much of past socialization regarding race was reinforced by art. Although more than ten percent of the U.S. population was black, there was an almost complete absence of blacks in American advertising before 1965. Caucasians did not particularly notice this absence. The absence was, in fact, a measure of their control of standards of attractiveness and patterns of consumption—a control so complete that the exclusive association of whiteness and beauty seemed more a law of nature than a deliberate policy of exclusion.

Many problems which cannot be worked out in the day-to-day social realm are "solved" in the aesthetic sphere. Artistic solutions range from the crudest sort of fantasy revenge to great imaginative exercises. The imaginative solution of the artist is simply a higher order of the same process routinely engaged in by oppressed groups and small children.

Children engage in elaborate power dreams that are given an additional change of form and direction by popular art. Compensatory power for the weakling is the heart of comic book appeal. Along with fantasy revenge against oppressors, it forms the bulk of motivation in juvenile escape fiction. The Crimson Avenger, Lieutenant Hercules, and The Steel Fist, with their towering statures and tiger muscles are easy masters of the galaxy. Youthful weakness and dependency is dissolved by their appalling strength.

Body-building advertisements regularly exploit these power fantasies. As a youngster with a very large, powerful older brother, I was an easy mark for George F. Jowett's thrilling invitation to become "big, brawny, rugged like the lordly oak" and to "throw off the yoke of weakness." His vivid tales of weaklings who had transformed themselves into powerfully muscled giants by means of his secret method set my pulse pounding. The reality of the course was more puzzling. I received a six pound set of oak leverage bells to be balanced in various swing positions. Charles Atlas was equally inspiring. He urged me to "gamble a stamp" and to turn the tables on bullies. The physical culture ads were more powerful than the comic book adventures, for the muscle builders had limited power. It was easier for me to identify with them. It was possible to implement the values for which they stood. One could actually enact the romance in a step-by-step, sequential mode. Yet, once even minimal results were achieved, the fantasy began to lose its glow. Nothing could match the tidy drama of the muscle picture books.

Those readers who grew up in rural protestantism especially know the art of the sermon which features a compensatory God who will ensure that the proud will be brought low and the virtuous exalted. A secular version of this sermon is the old, prairie radical oration of William Jennings Bryan in which the powerful are presented as the moral inferiors of the plain people. A society is envisioned in which the ordinary worker is exalted, and the oppressive parasite who rides upon the shoulders of the producers is humbled. Another variant is the old spiritual that opined: "Day after tomorrow coming with the bottom rail on the top."

There are several methods of reading the syntax of power in the mass media. This chapter will briefly discuss some of the major modes of analysis.

The Marxist Critique

Marxist analysis is self-confirming. It begins with the assumption that the mass media and the popular arts are weapons used by the dominant groups to maintain their power. Then, it seeks to discover ways in which newspapers, sports, television, painting, plays, movies, and novels both reflect and reinforce public acceptance of the authority of the dominant group. In America, Marxists maintain that the chief agents of enculturation are the mass media, rather than the formal educational systems. Furthermore, they argue that the socialization provided by the mass media is essentially an education in the legitimacy of authority.

As my earlier discussion of Marxist power theory indicated, alienation is the core concept. Alienation springs from the very nature of work in an industrial society. According to the romantic, Marxist version, craftsmen of earlier times produced a unique and individualized product, then came the industrial revolution. Its twin hammer blows of mass production and division of labor separated the craftsman's personality from the product. Mass production meant standardization of the product; division of labor divided the work process into parts and destroyed the worker's feelings of wholeness, control, mastery, and pride. Craftsmen were reduced to laborers. As the social, artistic, and fraternal relationships between worker and employer were crushed, only the economic relationship was left. Workers came to view themselves as commodities.

The role of the mass media under capitalism is to blunt the revolutionary energy of the workers by perverting the worker's desire for creative fulfillment and deep communion into an orgy of meaningless consumption. The worker is promised a bogus identity through the acquisition of consumer products. Thus, instead of revolting against exploitation by the master class, the worker seeks salvation by working harder than ever at his empty and deadening job so that he or she can acquire more and more products. Through this endless cycle of alienation, the worker becomes more and more frustrated and more and more of an isolated, competitive, and driven cipher. The mass media continually play upon the worker's deep insecurity, feelings of little worth, and fears of loneliness. They offer a bogus solution, as they constantly signal the worker to return to work in order to earn still more money for compensatory gratification, false identity, or orgiastic escape.

According to Marxist thought, Americans have been told to feel that their bodies are filthy, rotting masses of chemicals and that their odors and body faults must be constantly disguised, or they will be found out and ridiculed. The theorists point to the enormous sales of soaps and deodorants as proof that the engineered insecurity of the masses is a fact of life.

In addition to keeping the work force trapped on an endless treadmill of alienation, consumption, and work, the mass media have another role to play in shoring up the capitalist system. Marxists believe that the other task of the mass media is to keep the workers anxious, terrified, and confused; thus, if a worker tries to break out of the empty rituals of consumption in order to gain an understanding of the world, he or she cannot do so. The worker is confronted with an anarchy of titillating facts that astound without informing. Sensuous but opaque, the ever-shifting surfaces of American newspaper prose alternately terrify and sexually arouse the reader. Magazines parade an endless display of perversions and prodigies of nature. The packaged news of television's news stories socializes viewers to the dominant perceptual catagories and received ideas of the master class. They lack depth, real information, and nuance of any kind. Viewers are initially frightened and ultimately stultified.

Facts are ripped from an historical context that would give them meaning. Events are described from the perspective of the master class only. The pretense of objectivity is brayed forth in simplistic slogans: ''and that's the way it is...'' or ''the facts of the matter are these...'' and so on. Complex problems are presented as simple consequences of conditions that can be solved in a simple, finite way. In general, the function of such reporting is to discourage mobilization and to sew frustration, helplessness, and confusion. It ensures that the worker will not develop a world view (or even a coherent perspective) from which to challenge the existing arrangements of the social order.

If the worker turns to sports to escape from the crushing sense of victimization and alienation, he or she learns that the sports heroes and role models are, themselves, mere commodities. Athletes are bought and sold, whole teams are purchased, and coaches are dismissed at the drop of a hat. While not on the block or fighting legal battles, players are shills for products whose names they sometimes have difficulty pronouncing. Lacking team loyalty or any sense of communal belonging, these young statues of iron are shuttled from one arena to another until they become injured, lose their skills, or fall victim to Father Time. Meanwhile, they furnish valuable lessons for our children. Football, the most popular media sport of all, seems to have been made for television. It is almost pure form, thus it gives youth an education in dullness and regimentation. "Team players," as well as great "individuals," are rewarded, and the frenzy of the crowds illustrates the harmless siphoning off of potentially revolutionary elements.

According to Marxist critics, the "business dramas" of the 1980's socialize youth in a caricature of America's new capitalist man or woman. Youth sees a variety of manipulation techniques in a world in which everything is for sale, and people are treated as things. Heroes are appropriately competitive, continually measuring themselves against rivals, and looking over their shoulders at newcomers who are gnawing at the woodwork. The pseudo-participation in economic jungle warfare, and the endless rituals of over-consumption divert people from the misery and joylessness of their empty lives. For the Marxist, the very term "lifestyle" is a consumption marketing concept. It was invented by western social scientists (themselves hirelings of the syphilitic jackals of the Establishment) to distract the masses from thinking about ultimate questions. Mindless hedonism replaces the quest for justice and community.

According to Marxists, the American mass media are, at bottom, a grim and paranoid counterrevolutionary force, despite the "good buddy" style employed by them. No perversion of genuine public spirit is too degrading for American advertisers and, despite their slavish pandering to public taste, no heartfelt people's movement is sacred to them. The women's movement is used to sell a brand of cigarettes. Cheap, tawdry, and pornographic magazines are sold under a banner of gender liberation. One's most generous impulses — love and concern for one's children — are exploited by computer companies who terrify parents by warning them that their children will be left behind, unemployed, turned into the obsolete coolies of the new technocracy. Precisely the same appeal was used to sell encyclopedias for the past fifty years. The appeal to "skills education" has turned American universities into intellectual wastelands. American students are treated as consumers in primary and secondary education and are taught how to market themselves as commodities in higher education. Confused, undereducated, without historical perspective or philosophical grounding, their skills eroding under the pace of industrial change, these anxious new Americans have been rendered, in the words of Engels, "dead from the neck up."

Symbols are used in the most shameless and anxiety-producing ways. The security and self-satisfaction of the population must be systematically undermined so that they will seek secular salvation in the marketplace. The wish fulfillment logic of human greed must be exploited to produce public associations that are profitable, rather than rational. Thus, bottles of shampoo are shaped as medicine bottles with irrational juxtapositions of health, beauty, and youth.

Thus, according to Marxists, American television is not an adult medium, but rather, it is childish by design. The masters of America do not watch television. They have no need to watch the evening news, since they make it themselves. They are pleased by the ceaseless wheel of sitcoms, the reductive logic of the advertisements, and the apocalyptic glimpses of the newscasts, for this fare helps to reduce the lonely, detribalized American masses to a very primitive state. Without a sustaining culture or authoritative belief system, they are goaded by two things only: panic and greed. Advertisements generate mass anxiety and lower self-esteem. Sensationalistic journalism promotes numb terror, helplessness, and dependency. Sports events provide temporary distraction and socialize in dominant capitalist values. Mindless sitcoms exalt consumption heroes and ridicule any aspirations beyond amoral materialism. The list of examples goes on and on. The great weakness of this criticism is that it asserts a particular geography of power, and then goes on to confirm it through carefully selected examples. The worst of such analysis is a series of crudely etched stereotypes. The best swarms with unquestioned assumptions about the location and uses of power in western civilization.

Two Other Modes: The Freudian and the Semiotic

Despite the popularity of many logics of vision and new languages of art, there are only two other comprehensive analytic approaches besides that of the Marxists: the Freudian and the Semiotic. The Freudian, or symbolic, approach to graphics would interpret a popular advertisement for communications featuring lines of telephone poles marching across the American heartland as a display of upright male organs. The Semiotic, or non-symbolic, approach to graphics might read the same ad as one signalling the company's technological competence or its sense of order, restraint, and tidy mastery.

In contrast to the Marxian approach (essentially, a sociological perspective) and the Freudian (which reduces the messages of books, films, paintings, and television to a small vocabulary of latent psychological meanings), the Semiotic approach is one in which one deciphers a code.

While the Freudian looks for subliminal meanings, the Semiotician reads out the mosaic of surface meanings. The Freudian analysis is very powerful, but it is reductive and is limited by its restrictive categories and its traditional canons of interpretation. The Semiotic approach is not freighted with these categories. It assumes that one can read western civilization through its popular graphic media, just as one might "read out" a text. Semioticians believe that society signals itself through its human artifacts and through the composition of its recurrent images.

Let me illustrate through contrast. Recently, a Freudian and a Semiotician viewed a popular advertisement for an investment firm. This advertisement portrayed a wealthy elderly man flanked by a young man and a young woman, both immaculately groomed, new M.B.A.'s whose mouths were jammed with enormous white teeth. The trio strode up several flights of stairs, passing hunched chain-smoking men and women who slumped against the ballistrades or sat despairingly on the steps. As the elderly man spoke of the enormous opportunities of modern investment, the trio reached a large office door at the very top of the stairs and passed lightly and airily through the door. The Freudian analyst told me that ascending staircases symbolize sexual excitement, while the public entry into the office represents an incestuous entrance into the forbidden mother's secret chamber. The Semiotician was more prosaic. The steps symbolize hierarchy. People sit above one another in order of importance. There are rewards for the efforts of climbing; hence, the ascent of the trio represents social mobility or, perhaps, the ambitious and knowledgeable individual moving upward toward the central accounts of the business.

The two approaches yield vastly different results. In looking at a recruiting poster for the Armed Services, Freudian and Semiotic analysts "see" different messages. The short-haired, well-groomed young people are perceived in contrasting ways. The Freudian sees an erotic message—conspicuous hair is a covering for a sexual organ. For the Semiotician, short hair on men and pinned hair on women signal subjection to authority.

In earlier times, there was a union of the arts regarding vocabulary, symbology, and conventions. With the decline of the prestige of the classical heritage and the unifying power of Greco-Roman culture, this "language" has been lost. A brief digression here will provide some necessary historical density.

There once existed in the arts a mass of visual commonplaces, stock examples, templates, and themes. In the late Middle Ages and early Renaissance, there was a search for a rational basis for beauty. Apart from a language of power which took its syntax from religious doctrine, pagan mythology, and ancient European folklore, artists wanted an objective theory of proportion that would validate both the medieval belief in a harmonious cosmogony and the Renaissance hope for a universal mathematical principle. When these hopes could not be affirmed, artists seized upon Alberti's *exempeda*,[1] a series of characteristic social types. There remained many painterly conventions drawn from classical rhetoric. The medieval *allegory of prudence* both mimicked and celebrated Greco-Roman rhetoric in the three-headed symbol of prudential deliberation it had borrowed from Ancient Egypt. The *tricephalic image*[2] portrayed the combination of memory, judgment, and foresight in the decision-making process. In place of the Egyptian dog, lion, and wolf heads, European artists substituted three human heads: an old man looking backward into the past, searching out precedents for wise counsel based on the lessons of historical experience; a middle-aged man looking straight ahead, representing the ideal of human wisdom which deals with the immediate present by framing wise arguments based upon definition; and a beardless youth facing into the future, representing the ideal of foresight, the attempt to calculate the future consequences of several courses of action. Emblems and ideographs appear in painting from the thirteenth through the seventeenth centuries.

This common language, however, is no longer available to the general audience. In the present century, the visual and verbal mediums have diverged.[3] In rhetoric, the ethical commonplace book has been replaced by scientific method and by a study of the living materials of society. The old grammatical tradition of rhetoric, with its classical emphasis on balance, judgment, propriety, and adaptation has its limitations as a mode of analysis. The moving perspective of modern art, the emphasis on the process of "vision in motion"[4] and on light and form is opposed to the integrity of particular objects. These divergencies make the old verbal categories of analysis seem less adequate than ever.

The Semiotic Approach to Graphics

In the hands of an amateur, the Semiotic approach is a kind of intellectual Cuisinart, and its product a frothy meringue; however, registered European thinkers, such as Umberto Eco[5] and Roland Barthes,[6] demonstrate the sweep and beauty of this approach in their works.

Refusing to honor traditional distinctions between high art and the vulgar art forms of the masses, Semioticians have gravitated toward mass advertising, recruiting posters, fashion, and the popular arts by which the powerful routinely attempt to insinuate themselves upon ordinary people. Much Semiotic analysis is undertaken not for purposes of intellectual curiosity, but for the purpose of identifying and combating powerful groups. They reject traditional literary and artistic criticism because these forms of analysis treat artistic works as timeless, universal essences. They believe that traditional critics rip art from its historical context and ignore its function as a weapon of ideological dominance by the ruling groups.

Particularly for Barthes, criticism of the popular arts is a kind of name-calling or *ad hominem* argument. He skewers classical criticism savagely for repeating the function of myth. He believes that they throw dust in the eyes of the people by disguising political acts under utterly conventional acts or by concealing it under the guise of human nature. Even when viewing the great works of western literature and art, Barthes refuses to pay homage to the past, and "attempts a reconstruction of intelligibility for our own time."[7]

According to Barthes, every ruling group strives to make its dominance appear as a part of the natural order and, thus, to be accorded primacy with as little resistance as would be made to the law of gravity or the pressure of air. To this end, it uses the arts to propagate its reigning image; its ascendancy is incarnated in art. Its art is concealed in conventional forms. The dominant class has an official language, a language so unlike the dialect of the array of local and provincial groups that it appears transparent, universal, timeless. Its power is concealed in conventionality.

Barthes' favorite example of this concealment is the famous French recruiting poster (no longer seen since Metropolitan France has been shorn of its subject peoples). This poster was the last pretentious gasp of France as a world culture, a universal nation, and as the bearer of light to developing peoples lost in darkness. The poster features a pair of smiling African and Asiatic (former French Indo-Chinese) soldiers erect and saluting against a landscape of French Normandy blondes. Flying above them is an enormous French tricolor. A huge ghost image of the flag is superimposed on the whole scene. According to Barthes, the picture is merely another bid for the French ruling classes (the managerial bourgeoisie) to maintain their economic and social advantages, the poster's message being: this salute by African colonials and Asiatic clients is the most natural thing in the world, and their affection for France is as spontaneous as that of a youth born on the stormy beaches of Normandy. France is more than a nation, more than a parochial political division of Western Europe, more than an accidental fusion of Gallo-Roman and Teutonic tribes, more than a dynastic and geographic accident. France is an idea. It is a progressive revelation of human potential and freedom. One must be born in Germany to be a German; only native Italians can be Italians; and distinctions are hard and fast between "true-born Englishmen" and those recent arrivals who were born under bluer skies. Anyone can become a Frenchman, however, simply by embracing the French ideal of civilization. After all, the whole world wants to be French in thought, language, and sentiment. The unfolding vision of France transcends race, ethnicity, geography, and social class. France is the spirit that has gone abroad in the world to bring the gifts of Democracy, Meritocracy, Commerce, and the Arts to all those who are enveloped in darkness. Barthes assumes that his readers will laugh scornfully. The scales will fall from their eyes at the moment he identifies the self-interest and parochial aspiration of the bourgeoisie as the hidden inspiration of the drawing. According to Barthes, the popular arts are the arena in which the ruling classes use myth to disguise culture as nature:

> Myth consists in overturning culture into nature or at least the social, the cultural, and the ideological into the natural.... What is nothing but a product of class division and its moral, social, and aesthetic consequences is presented (stated) as being a matter of course; under the effect of inversion the quite contingent foundations of the utterance become Common Sense, Right Reason, the Norm, General Opinion.... [8]

Those who find class dominance a fruitful perspective in the study of graphics might do well to study Barthes. He supplies a vocabulary, an ideological perspective and a sense of mission for the scholar of mass media. Barthes calls the text a policeman, likening it to a censor or traffic controller. For Barthes, the printed text has "repressive value," [9] or it has deleted some meanings of the image and fixed others. He names the functions of the linguistic message "anchorage" and "relay." [10] The term anchorage refers to the power of a linguistic message to add clarity to a visual image and to help fix its meaning. Images are ambiguous; they have too many meanings, and we must look to the print below the picture to know which meanings are relevant and significant. Anyone who has ever watched a movie at a distance without the benefit of sound or gesticulating people, has experienced the frustration of trying to choose between a multitude of interpretations. Uncertain and ambiguous signs arouse terror and anxiety. Relay, the other function of the text, is the closure that language provides. The "hot" text takes the amorphous emotions and desires aroused by the visual image and channels them into action. It links the affective fantasy of the text to the world of day-to-day behavior; thus, popular arts can serve as commands to vote, purchase, believe, join, act, or march.

The ideological roots of Barthes' theory, which is that of an outsider, are readily apparent. Barthes tells us that his sense of estrangement is great due to a number of reasons, including the fact that he was born a Protestant in a country where it is natural to be a Catholic. [11] Similarly, the death of his father, his fall from wealth to genteel poverty, the deflection from his projected career path, and, finally, a lifelong illness separated him from the robust life of his class. Even his professional success was cankered by the feeling that he now occupied an elite post without the usual academic credentials. Further, he began as a classical scholar, but blunted his sensibility by immersing himself in the analysis of commercials, comic strips, and fashion magazines. He felt guilt in the enjoyment of literature and in the many ways in which his success prevented him from proclaiming solidarity with the underclass. In short, he had precisely those traits of the continental intellectual that make him or her seem pretentious and a little absurd to North Americans.

Aside from the ideological baggage that led Barthes to his insight, his idea of advertising's power as a product of the interaction of its linguistic and visual messages is valuable.

The Power of Modern Advertising:
The Interanimation of Text and Image

Modern advertising is a powerful institution. Some scholars feel it represents a distillation of modern Western culture. Since the modern West has eschewed social control through overt coercion, it is deeply committed to obtaining consent through constant manipulation. The most overt manifestation of this occurs in its free-choice economic arrangements buttressed by a forty billion dollar industry—advertising.

Advertising provides an enormous richness and density of material for those who wish to study mass persuasion as it operates at the intersection of broadcasting, marketing, literature, and art. Here, to use Barthes' vocabulary, text and vision are merged in millions of finite and episodic persuasive attempts. Further, as a multi-media form (in a society that is saturated with and dominated by mass media culture), commercial advertising represents a starker, one might almost say a purer, model of persuasion than the old-fashioned models of persuasion drawn from the oratory of our courts and the deliberations of our legislatures. Until the twentieth century, our notions of persuasive argument and the engineering of mass consent were drawn from classical oratory and the high periods of British and American forensic debate. Mass advertising bursts the restrictions of logical rigor, relevant evidence, and informed rebuttal. In an unabashed way, it employs myth, archetype, allegory, and religious vision for the often puny purpose of encouraging a huge number of rudimentary transactions. God, human freedom, equality, and community are invoked to sell light bulbs, toilet paper and napkins. In this sense, it spans all cultural boundaries, a holy discourse in the service of the most mundane and secular ends. Advertising offers identity, affiliation, psychic energy, liberation from fear, and love through the medium of commercial exchange. It invests inherently dull subjects—soap, razor blades and towels—with "huge cloudy symbols of high romance."

Of course, it may be said that commercial advertising, despite its pervasive vulgarity and unmitigated crassness, provides one of the few arenas in which ordinary people are able to operationalize their personal values. In an increasingly rationalized, lonely, and secular society, even a small, and perhaps illusory, personal choice may contribute to the stability and psychic health of our communities.

Advertising works through merger. It forges a connection between the external world of affairs and the private world of wishes and fantasies. The act of purchase becomes the means by which one operationalizes one's values, expresses one's personal aesthetic, enacts one's deepest beliefs, asserts one's identity. Raw desire, need for belongingness, and fear of loss are its levers of persuasion. Ordinary pedestrian logic means little. Advertisers believe that American men hunger for male identity, but the primary badges of that identity are archaic, nineteenth-century occupations such as hewing down trees, herding cattle, breaking horses, and mountain-style, no-holds-barred grappling on cinder pits. It is difficult to enact these masculine rituals in a twentieth-century, technological, information-oriented society; thus, the rituals must be enacted analogically or metaphorically. Gun manufacturers sell weapons to city dwellers using agrarian or wilderness appeals. The city is seen as the new wilderness, the frontier, or the jungle. Chainsaw and pickup truck can be presented as the moral equivalents of axe and horse.

Advertisers depend upon eye as well as ear, because advertising is (as mentioned earlier) almost entirely composed of dull subjects. Automobiles, clothing, and houses are subjects in which there is a steady and intense interest. To be sure, people do seek out information about them; however, most advertising revenues come from prosaic objects such as batteries, mouthwash, and hand lotion. These objects must be connected to the consumer's vision of the good life. Here is where Barthes' idea is insightful, for every subject must be expanded mythically and charged with emotion through dramatic imagery and rich visual associations. Then, it must be closed down through the hot, finite, specific, and concrete use of language.

Consequently, a successful; i.e., powerful ad needs a visual text and verbal text. The visual image is implicit, mythic, and energizing. It evokes childhood, the haunted past, racial memory, buried ideals, nameless fears, unrealized aspirations and dreams. Its emotional tug is stinging sharp and, at the same time, deep as the roots of the race. The verbal text is hot and specific. It is a vector of force channeling and directing the image into a resolution, an explicit and limited act.

In this way, a commercial product is presented as a synecdoche—a part that stands for the whole. The purchase of a backpack allows the consumer to affirm an outdoor lifestyle or to participate in a return to nature. A decade ago, an ad told young women that, by adding blond highlights to their hair, they were making a commitment to a fuller life.

The vision or image contained in an advertisement is emotionally overpowering and, like most images, very heavily freighted with information. It is, of course, too full of information to be useful to the sponsor who cannot depend upon the consumer to select the commercially relevant message. That is why the verbal text (either by print or voice) is vitally necessary. It tells the consumer what to focus upon in the vision, how to participate in the vision, and how the purchase will operationalize the visual message. The vision smashes the secular world and provides a glimpse of paradise or hell. The verbal text directs the audience's response toward a specific and commercially profitable response.

This concept of the interaction of visual and verbal dimensions of an ad to produce response is not unlike a theory of the way in which metaphor works which was put forward by Ivor Armstrong Richards, the distinguished British literary critic.[12] According to Richards, a metaphor works because it is both familiar and strange. Two literally false but psychologically compatible ideas are brought together in a cognitive frame. If the semantic distance between the two concepts is too great, they will not snap together in a flash of insight for the hearer or reader. The metaphor will fall apart; it will be opaque or obscure. It will not serve the reader as a metaphor, but rather will provide darkness instead of insight. "England as New Jerusalem" and "work as prayer" have served as powerful galvanizing metaphors at various times in history. Most metaphoric expressions ("the lip of the cup," "as strong as an ox," etc.) quickly fade and die.

In a similar way, the visual and verbal parts of a text must work together. The fantastic claims of the verbal text cannot render the vision ridiculous. An advertisement must have some claim to credibility if it is to invite participation. Of course, whether it works or not depends very much on the desire, desperation, or options of the beholder and not upon objective logical criteria. A dying acquaintance once enthusiastically sent in for a mail-order cure that he would have laughed at a few months earlier. The aesthetic and psychological satisfactions of a purchase cannot be separated from its pragmatic advantages. Traditional wisdom once affirmed, the higher the cost of a product, the smaller part irrational and aesthetic factors play in a decision to purchase.

In a famous study of consumer behavior, it was found that consumers did not purchase laundry products for reasons of economy, performance, or health. One fabric softener was not preferred over another because of its superior efficacy in killing germs; rather, the fabric softener that drew a response from family members because of its sweet scent was preferred. It satisfied the most powerful and fundamental need, approval—a need that outstripped the so-called pragmatic needs.

Why is advertising (and, indeed, all the popular arts) a source of potential power today? It is because, through the aesthetic of advertising, the masses experience the same momentary wholeness of instinct, mind, body, and spirit that the "higher arts" bestowed on the world-weary elites of centuries past. A body-building ad suggests the journey of the questing hero of earlier tribal experiences. At the core of human religious experience is the heroic journey (separation and shame, initiation and passage to a new world through arcane exercises, routines and trials, and finally, transcendence and return with the gifts of the gods). In modern body-building, the salvation is entirely secular; the body, rather than the ego, is mastered, and the "gifts" are merely increased bulk, strength, and intense vascularity. Yet, something is given. The gifts may be illusory, but all human victories are Pyrrhic victories. To ask more is to cry out for the gifts a secular, over-organized, mass-mediated society cannot give.

Notes

[1]Erwin Panofsky, "The History of the Theory of Human Proportion as a Reflection of Styles," in *Meaning in the Visual Arts* (Garden City, NY: Doubleday, 1957), pp. 55-107.

[2]E. Panofsky and F. Saxl, "A Late Antique Religious Style in Works by Holbein and Titian," *Burlington Magazine,* XLIX, 1926, 177ff.

[3]Does painting have an inventional process corresponding to the traditional generative categories and argumentative forma (topoi) found in rhetoric? Is the relationship between an audience and an artist similar to that of the rhetor and his or her constituents? It would seem so. Despite the philosophical and religious justifications of many artists, the power of audience validation — that which seems right in the eye of the beholder — has triumphed over what is "objectively right again and again." See Horst de La Croix and Richard G. Taney, *Gardner's Art Through the Ages,* 6th ed. (New York: Harcourt, Brace and Janovich, Inc., 1975), p. 534. See also pages 433 and 434. For an example of rhetorical borrowings in the painterly medium, see Joshua Reynolds, *Discourses* (esp. 13 and 15) in *World's Classics* (Oxford: Oxford University Press, 1907).

[4]See L. Moholy Nagy, *Vision in Motion* (Chicago: Paul Theobold and Co., 1956).

[5]The most comprehensive statement in Umberto Eco's *A Theory of Semiotics,* (Bloomington, Indiana: University of Indiana Press, 1976). For an ingenious application, see Preface to the British Edition of Umberto Eco's novel, *The Name of the Rose*, trans. by William Weaver (London edition, New York: Harcourt, Brace and Janovich, Inc., 1981), p. xi.

[6]The most panoramic view of Barthes' work is in the collection of his essays called *Image, Music, Text* (New York: Hill and Wang, 1977). The best exposition is George Wasserman's *Roland Barthes* (Boston: Twayne Publications, 1981).

[7]Barthes, *Image, Music, Text,* p. 165.

[8]Ibid., p. 50.

[9]Ibid., p. 40.

[10]Ibid.

[11]George Wasserman, *Roland Barthes* (Boston: Twayne Publications, 1981), p. 16.

[12]See Ivor Armstrong Richards, *Philosophy of Rhetoric* (New York: Oxford University Press, 1941).

9

Historical Conceptions of Power

In every society of which we have knowledge, power is distributed unevenly. It has always been so. Historically, every society has been hierarchical. In some cases, power has been held by naked force; in other societies, power has been freely granted to leaders whose authority was accepted as right and legitimate. The verdict of history is that all power is unstable. Great leaders are constantly overthrown, and the most secure dynasties lose coherence and crumble away. The children of heroes are degenerates. Dominant classes are replaced or subordinated by new conquerors.

Power is not only exhibited in conflict. The exercise of power is as necessary to human cooperation as it is to savage competition. Then, too, acts of power are shot through with ethical considerations. All human actions have consequences, and these effects can be judged either good or evil. Some uses of power have immensely productive consequences. Other uses of power produce the most abominable evils.

These characteristics — instability, cooperative necessity, and an inescapable moral dimension — have caused people to think systematically about power. Not surprisingly, power theorists have appeared as action leaders at least as often as they have been retired intellectuals. Furthermore, theories of power have seldom been disinterested descriptions of human behavior. Often, they have been thinly disguised political action programs.

The historical review of power theories contained in this chapter is far from complete. On the other hand, it is extensive enough to suggest some of the richness and diversity of power theory in Western thought.

Early Conflict Theorists: The Sophists and Plato

Many early theories of power are conflict theories. The fundamental axiom of conflict theory is that trials of strength are the great creative forces of history. Many early conflict theorists believed that competition is a greater spur to human excellence than cooperation. George Bryan Vold, the eminent American criminologist and one of the great modern conflict theorists, calls conflict theory "the grunt and groan theory of historical development."[1]

One of the earliest conflict theorists was the Greek philosopher, Heraclitus of Ephesus (c. 500 B.C.). Fascinated by the unceasing changes he observed in nature, he came to believe that nature was the father and the mother of all things. To illustrate his belief in constant flux, he is supposed to have affirmed that "one can never step in the same river twice." For Heraclitus, all social and physical change is accomplished through a kind of mystical transformation. In the course of this pre-Hegelian dialectic, everything is changed into its opposite through struggle, and then led back toward its old identity.

The belief that conflict is the generative engine of human culture echoes down the corridors of the centuries. Many evolutionary theories were based on a belief in the adaptive and progressive consequences of competition. The popular slogan, "survival of the fittest" encapsulated this idea and was used to justify some of the more lurid adventures of European colonial expansion. Moreover, this idea underlaid the pronouncement of liberal economists that free competition resulted in better and cheaper products.

Conflict is the key ingredient in Karl Marx's class struggle. According to Marx, the engine of social improvement is a "just war" to end exploitation, greed, and inequality forever. As a matter of fact, conflict is seen as a key factor even by those who hate conflict and wish to end it permanently.

A variation of conflict theory, "the right of the stronger" or "might makes right" was held by certain of the sophists, a group of wandering teachers in ancient Athens (4th and 5th centuries B.C.). Polus, a pupil of the famous sophist, Gorgias, and Callicles, a wealthy Athenian citizen, argued with Socrates' belief in the cultivation of virtue. They maintain that power, not virtue or enlightenment, is the greatest gift of mankind. For these sophists, the highest attainment of the individual is the ability to terrify and dominate others. Morality, according to Callicles, is a conspiracy hatched by the many weaklings in order to dominate the few strong. Duty, justice, and compassion are inventions of the weak to make the strong ashamed to use their strength.

An ingenious variation of this doctrine is put into the mouth of Thrasymachus in Plato's *Republic.* Thrasymachus argues that "the interest of the stronger" is a phrase that describes the end of every government. He turns the idea of Callicles on its head. Now, government is presented as an invention of the strong to oppress the weak. The strong consolidate their power in a government in order to stabilize it and to give it a facade of legitimacy. Furthermore, the use of government to oppress the weak is justified because, Thrasymachus tells us, there is no such thing as general welfare or higher public good. He expresses the belief that human beings are fundamentally estranged from one another. Identity of interests between the people and the state is an attractive fraud. Thus, even though it routinely invokes the sanction of God, the People, History, and the Common Good in support of its acts, government only masquerades as an instrument of the entire community. In fact, according to this point of view, it is really a partisan weapon of the elite to oppress the common people.

Thrasymachus' position transcends amoral individualism. His fundamental premise is one that is met with again and again in Western thought—the belief that all human beings are alienated by nature. The goals that individuals pursue—however strongly they are felt to be personal aspirations—are never completely their own. We are social beings, who, by nature, are involved in a complex web of individual and communal relationships. Furthermore, our atomized individualism is a modern phenomenon. Neither Plato nor Thrasymachus could imagine a truly human life outside the intense semi-tribal world of the polis. On the other hand, even in the most collectivist community, the ends of a single individual are never completely identical with those of anyone else. This basic conflict of ends, the secular mark of Cain, mandates that the powerful must seek their own ends and neglect those of others.

Many revolutionaries, including Karl Marx, have agreed with the spirit of Thrasymachus' conception of government. A common revolutionary argument is that governments are merely the tools of the propertied classes. The state is seen as the repressive apparatus of the owner's of the community wealth-making resources. Of course, Marx greatly extends Thrasymachus' dominance argument by affirming that the legal, religious, philosophical, and artistic life of the community form a single cultural weapon to propagandize the ideas of the dominant group and fasten them upon the masses.

Another kind of conflict theory is that of Plato[2] (427-347 B.C.). For Plato, intellect is the scarce resource; thus, a monopoly of intelligence and a control of the sources of information ensure the dominance of an intellectual elite. Plato's method of arriving at truth is a routinized conflict of ideas, the dialectic.

Plato's theory is embodied in his elegantly written dialogues and, most particularly, in his program for the ideal society, *The Republic.* The

Republic of Plato, that perfect and changeless utopia managed by Philosopher-Kings, is emphatically not a democracy. Power is not vested in the people; it is located in a carefully nurtured intellectual elite. This elite has two tasks in regard to the lower orders. The first is to train them to do their jobs. The second is to prevent them from learning things that would distract them from their duty. Plato does not believe in educating people beyond their capacity. In one of his most famous dialogues ("The Gorgias"), he has Socrates break off the dispute with Callicles on the grounds that he is uneducable.

The elite have other duties as well. They dispense justice, allocate the wealth in common, evaluate the talents and worth of all other citizens, assign them functions and "places" within the state, command the soldier caste, and lead the whole community to the realization of the Good. In short, every detail of public and private life is to be overseen by them.

Plato argues for the moral excellence of this particular distribution of power through an elaborate series of analogies. One of these analogies compares the metals gold, silver, and brass to the different sorts of natures people possess. The Philosopher-Kings possess golden natures, the soldier caste silver, the workers brass or, perhaps, even iron or lead.

The use of metals to suggest an order of virtue among human souls is based upon the ancient idea of correspondences. According to this idea, everything in the natural world corresponds to or partakes of something in the spirtual world, yoked together as microcosm and macrocosm. The ship in the harbor is an imperfect realization of the archetypal ship in the spiritual world. The justice of the civic court is but an imperfect earthly version of divine justice. Qualities and functions, as well as objects, demonstrate correspondence. A ceiling or a wall is not a fixed entity. Rotate a wall 90 degrees, and it becomes a ceiling; rotate the same ceiling 180 degrees, and it becomes a floor. Ceilings, walls, and floors are not things but functions, forms drawn from an invisible blueprint derived from an ideal world that exists beyond the world of the physical senses. We have never seen a perfectly straight line or an exact triangle, but the idea is in our minds because straight lines and perfect triangles exist in an ideal realm. We call our imperfect renderings of these figures "triangles" or "lines" because they represent or correspond to these perfect archetypes. Thus it is that objects like ships, qualities like justice or mercy, functions like walls, and relationships such as mathematical formulas transcend material existence. They are fully realized in the ideal world.

The ideal world is not merely a realm of ideas, functions, patterns, and relationships. It is a hierarchy, a moral order in which some things are higher, better, and more significant than others. The ideal world of Plato is an order of goods. The forms in the natural world that correspond to a particular good "participate" in that good at a particular level in the hierarchy. Thus, ideal justice is a relationship of perfect equality of treatment under comparable conditions. The actual justice accorded to Socrates at Athens was only a shadowy reflection of the perfect transcendent "Justice" of the ideal order. Because of this link, even the shabby and imperfect justice of the Athenian courts merits our compliance and our loyalty. However imperfectly, it is informed by the higher justice of the spiritual world.

Similarly, in Plato's Republic, some individuals attain more virtue than others. The Philosopher-Kings have golden natures. These persons have a clear perception of spiritual reality, the ultimate good. They can divine truth from lies, discern appearance from reality, and distinguish between love and lust. Because of their great clarity of perception, they are the natural leaders of the community. Next on the ladder of human hierarchy are those who possess silver natures. They cannot directly apprehend the true nature of things, but they can understand divine truth when they have been instructed in it by the golden-natured Philosopher-Kings. They are the natural protectors of the elite, forming the silver-natured soldier caste. Below the soldier caste are those who correspond to less precious metals such as bronze, copper, iron, or lead. They cannot be instructed in higher matters, but are often well-disposed, if they are firmly guided in right action and set to work at useful pursuits. These baser metal natures are easily deceived by cunning sophists or seduced by promiscuous artists. If left to their own government, they will consult only their appetites and their passions. If there are any iron or lead natures in the community, they must be firmly guided, for their darkened minds hardly rise above the level of beasts. The better the earthly community, the more faithfully will it reflect the hierarchical order of the ideal world.

In speaking of his ideal community, Plato uses the metaphor of the human soul, an entity he considers to be divided into three parts: intellect, will, and passion. In the well-ordered soul, the intellect is firmly in command, the will is its instrument, and the passions are subordinated and directed toward right action. In the disordered soul, the passions are predominant. When the passions rule, the intellect degenerates into a cunning little engine, and the will becomes feeble and vicious.

The metaphor of the divided soul is not unique to Plato. It reappears throughout the history of European thought, serving as the basis for Aristotle's modes of persuasion (rational, emotional, and social), and emerging once more in Freud's ego, superego, and id. Likewise, it is the basis of Marx's tripartite class struggle (workers, bourgeoisie, and intellectuals). It is a model which is continually rediscovered, and, because it represents an integral part of our human nature, it is at the root of our most basic interpersonal interactions, such as extended dialogues between parents and children.

For Plato, society is the soul writ large. The well-ordered society is one whose class structure reflects the dominance of intellect over will and passion. In the good society, intellectuals are in firm control of all channels of communication, of the allocation of goods and services, and of the system of education—in fact, of every facet of the decision-making process. The soldiers (corresponding to the Will) are loyal subjects of the Philosophers, assuring their safety and providing them a monopoly on the means of physical coercion. Lastly, the workers (corresponding to the passions), are taught what they must know to perform their tasks and are protected from everything that they do not need to know. In order to protect the workers from false beliefs, neither dramatists nor rhetoricians are allowed in the Republic. These mountebanks (corresponding to our advertisers and media writers) deal with appearances rather than truth. According to Plato, they rouse the passions of the people for mere aesthetic effect or for personal advantage—never for the common good. The individualism and relativism of these artists subvert the state. In order to deal with these charlatans, Plato allows the guardians of the state the authority to practice censorship freely. Theatre is not permitted, for it often depicts evil in an attractive guise. The debates of the rhetoricians are not allowed since virtue is a settled question articulated by an elite which speaks with a single voice. One does not, according to Plato, need tolerance of other people's opinions if one already has the truth.

By banning even the expression of challenges to the established order, Plato's state provides no mechanism for social change. Justice consists of knowing your place and staying in it. The shoemaker makes shoes, the farmer plows and reaps, the dockworker lifts and hauls, the soldier drills and fights, and the Philosopher-King governs.

Plato's model of power distribution is not a bizarre aberration. It is the most common model of communal government in the history of the world. Governments by the consent of the people have been rare and fleeting. States run by tiny disciplined elites have been the rule. This is the case even in the West where, during the Middle Ages, celibate priestly castes with a monopoly on administrative skills held power. In many modern socialist states, party members, the intelligentsia, technocrats, and other holders of specialized knowledge make most of the significant decisions.

Setting aside the particular rigidity of Plato's model, it is easy to see that it illustrates a principle that is at work throughout social life: power gravitates to the holder of the scarce resource. In a land-based community, power settles in the hands of the propertyholders. In a technocracy, decision-making authority becomes the province of technocrats. In a capitalistic order, power gravitates, either formally or informally, toward those holders of capital who know how to use money to create new wealth and jobs; that is, capitalists. For Plato, the scarce resource is a special kind of intellect, a special kind of human insight that perceives the nature of the Good. Fortunately, morality and intellect coincide in Plato's concept of the universe. He believes that evil is a product of ignorance. As insight produces psychological health for Freud, wisdom produces virtue for Plato. The criminal who came to know the nature and consequences of crime would cease to be a criminal.

What about Greek democracy, that Athenian invention so powerfully celebrated by Pericles in his Funeral Oration, a tribute that has outlasted the language in which it was uttered? What does Plato think about a system where power is located in the body of the people and only loaned to leaders for specified periods? In Plato's *Phaedrus*, Socrates compares democracy to a storm-tossed ship in which the terrified occupants gather to choose a captain. They vote to reject a sober, nondescript man who has a genuine knowledge of navigation and, rather, to elect a charming, popular fellow whose gait and manner inspire confidence. The elected dandy really knows nothing whatever about seamanship. He promptly steers the ship onto the rocks, smashing it utterly.

Plato's most decisive and bitter verdict against democracy is delivered in his famous parable of the cave. The story's lesson: democracy is rule by a mob — the same Athenian mob that murdered the wisest, the best, and the most beloved Philosopher-King of all, Socrates. In the Myth of the Cave, Plato leaves us a moving tale of the fate of his master in Athens.

In Plato's tale, we are asked to imagine a group of people seated on the edge of a low trench in an underground cave. These people are chained together so tightly that they cannot turn around and can barely glance to the right or left. Behind them, completely hidden from their view, are their captors and guardians in the rear of the cave. There, the guardians have built a large bright fire which casts fantastic patterns of light and shadow on the front wall of the cave. The prisoners observe these light projections and see "pictures" made by the fire. The fire pictures become the basis of elaborate stories. The stories are polished, standardized, and, finally, fitted into an ambitious system of thought. The system becomes a key to interpreting the meaning of life. The stories explain how the people came to be present in the cave, how they should conduct themselves while there, and whither they are going afterward. In short, a complete cosmogony was developed from the reflections of firelight on a cave wall.

The cosmogony of the people is vastly amusing to the guardians. They find the situation richly comic, with one exception. They find the speech of the wisest of their captives, a man called Socrates, oddly perceptive. One day, they decide to take him apart from the others and enlighten him. He is unchained. He is shown the fire as the source of the images. He is taken above-ground, where he sees earth, grass, flowing water, trees waving together in the wind, the fiery disc of the Sun, clouds, spattering rain, flowers, singing birds, tall, shouldering mountains, and wine-dark sea. Socrates is so overwhelmed by this assault on his senses that, at first, he can only roll on the ground in fright and steal glances at the bumbling, tossing confusion. Gradually, he begins to sort out the sights and sounds and is able to form a coherent image of his new surroundings. After a time, he is able to stand erect and marvel at the soft, azure sky, the rain-freighted clouds, and the miracle of the grass. Socrates has looked upon the face of actual nature, and he can never again be contented with the delusions of the cave fires. The guardians take him back to the cave, however, and chain him once again in his old place on the bank of the shallow trench. Amused by the childish stories of the people, he begins at once to tell them of the true origins of the shifting fire picture. At first, they are stupified, then irritated, and, finally, outraged by his account of a world beyond the cave. "Impious liar," they shout, and strangle him with their manacles. The mob kills Socrates for uttering a truth they cannot comprehend. This is democracy for Plato, a rule by numbers, a pooling of massive ignorance, a celebration of mass appetite by stupid mountebanks who follow rather than lead. When it does not end in violence, it oppresses inquiry by mass intimidation, a process not unlike the feather-showing ritual used by large birds to intimidate small ones.

Power as Human Organization: Early Theorists

Other early theorists stressed man's capacity for cooperation as the source of power. They were less impressed by the audacity and magnetism of rival generals than by the disciplined military organizations at their disposal. Pericles does not infuse a new spirit into the Athenians to rally them against the Spartan foe; he merely rouses the spirit that has been nurtured by the collective body of the polis. It is not that we admire Caesar's biceps and deltoids, but rather his understanding of the strengths and weaknesses of the Roman government and Roman military organization.

One who was more impressed with cooperation than conflict as a source of human dominion was that great student of human community, Aristotle (384-322 B.C.). This encyclopedic-minded philosopher inherited a vast body of unsolved problems from his master, Plato. Among these were the problems of governance. Instead of constructing an ideal state, Aristotle categorized types of states from the communities of the world around him. At one point, he collected and examined 171 different constitutions. Although he could not conceive of anyone leading a full human existence outside the Greek polis, Aristotle's theory of power tends to be descriptive rather than programmatic.

In his treatise on politics, Aristotle classifies states according to their ecology of power. The location of power within a community determines the character and outlook of the poeple, as well as the stability of their community. Aristotle's classification according to the geography of power is familiar to us. In a monarchy, power is located in a single person or dynastic family; in an oligarchy, it is located in a single class or aristocracy; in a democracy, power is spread widely among the people. In order to use power effectively, those in power have to be sure of regular compliance to their authority. To depend upon naked coercion or savage conflict is both costly and ultimately ineffective. Rulers who have to depend upon constant violence end up smashing the very human and material resources they wish to control. Power has to be seen as legitimate by those under its sway. Aristotle notes that legitimation is, ultimately, a rhetorical process. Authority is obeyed because people are convinced or "persuaded" that it rests upon a deeply held belief. Consensual communal belief underlay power, and that belief can be appealed to whenever its authority to act is challenged.

For example, in a monarchy, power is legitimated through the monarch's claim to superior blood, connection with divinity, or descent from revered ancestors. The erosion of these beliefs among the people strikes directly at the monarch's claims to legitimacy. Similarly, an aristocracy anchors its appeal to legitimacy in its blood lines, in hereditary prerogatives, in a proud connection with the birth of the community, or in any number of past events, as long as they are held to be convincing or decisive in the minds of the people. In a democracy, a ruler points to the performance of certain acts (election by a majority), to continued service to the people, or to a host of communal benefits gained while serving as an agent of the people.

According to Aristotle, each form of government has its own life cycle and its particular vulnerability. A believer in the shaping power of institutional and aesthetic form upon human behavior, Aristotle affirms that each kind of government (power locus) produces a characteristic personality type. Together with his observations on the effect of demographic factors such as sex, age, social class, education, and religion on audience response, Aristotle's insights into governance provide a guide for the statesman and the political orator.[3]

Elsewhere, Aristotle takes up the problem of values. Every community possesses a hierarchy of values (whether it articulates them or not) by which its agenda of acts is justified. Accordingly, acts of power take place within a context of community goals. Power is never meaningful in an abstract or potential form. The fundamental question is: "Power in the service of what end?"

Aristotle believes that there is a general progression of communal ends. This progression moves from the satisfaction of animal necessities toward the full realization of the good life. A responsible use of power travels this path. This art of politics seeks first to satisfy the basic necessities of the community. Then, when the community has solved the basic difficulties of getting food, shelter, and physical security, it necessarily moves to the next goal. The next goal is the flowering of the arts. When the community begins to enjoy a rich cultural life, a new and still higher, stage must be sought.

During this new stage, the citizens must take a genuine role in the management of the governance of the state. After political life attains maturity, leisure and philosophy are possible. Now comes the last stage, in which a religion emerges that forges a strong link between public morality and personal conduct. To accommodate this need, Aristotle envisages a refurbishing of Greek religion by which the gods lost their anthropomorphic character and find their abode in the visible heavens.

Aristotle's cooperative ethic makes massive demands on the citizenry as the price for the responsible use of power. He sees them full of sympathetic understanding for the self-interest of other citizens and even able to set aside their own self-interest for the sake of a higher communal good.

Reason, for the sophists, makes the individual more formidable. It is a dissolvent of convention and a liberator of "superior" people from social custom. For Aristotle, reason is an engine for human cooperation. It is a bulwark of consensus which brings order. Aristotle's ideal community is a society in which power is no longer a divisive issue, but a collective engine for the attainment of the good life.

Another theorist of organizational power was Marcus Tullius Cicero (106-43 B.C.), spokesman for the Roman Republic in its stormiest years and, perhaps, the greatest practitioner of persuasion in the ancient world. Rome's greatest orator, writer, and lawyer, Cicero rose from relative obscurity to Rome's highest office. He built his influence on a great substructure of favors, alliances, obligations, and bargains.[4]

Cicero's political treatise, *De Republica*, is not very informative of his actual practices and, thus, reveals almost nothing about how Cicero attained power. Like so many of his works on oratory and virtue, it deals with ideal rather than with actual factors. Cicero's method of amassing power through a network of social exchanges is detailed in his personal letters, more than 900 of which have survived. Cicero, the only middle-class individual of his time to gain the supreme office of Consul, was the patron of a large group to whom he gave legal aid, preferment, practical advice, and occasional direct favors. He was the candidate of the equestrian class and the banking community, a powerful constituency lacking any other formal representation. This newly risen group had a broader involvement in the vast colonial domains, a more cosmopolitan outlook, and potentially greater resources than the old aristocracy. This class had gained power outside the old framework of the Roman city-state, an entity that retained provincial loyalties along with antiquated machinery, and which was, thus, wholly inadequate to govern the new territories acquired by the army. The financial community backed Cicero in the hope of gaining political influence commensurate with its economic role.

During his rise, Cicero insinuated himself into the favor of those persons who might be useful to him. Even after his fall from power, he was still doing it by habit and reflex. Unfortunately, he backed the wrong horse. He believed that General Pompey would rout the forces of Gaius Julius Caesar. Caesar's victory resulted in years of forced retirement for him, although it gave him time to produce the enduring works that justified his life.

Cicero is a splendid example of the maxim: "It's not what you know, but who you know that counts."[5] Students who want to get ahead through the human network would do well to study his letters. They remind one of the Harvard Business School dean who was supposed to have remarked that his students learned a little accounting, management, and economic theory, but, most importantly, they learned to know each other. On the other hand, it is well to remember that a career built upon patronage probably worked better in the Greco-Roman world than it would in the mobile, fragmented, and atomized society of today. If business in the modern world is in some sense still a social system, in Ancient Rome it was very much a tribal system. Sponsorship, mentoring, and patronage were not seen as optional techniques or good policies. They were expected norms of behavior.

Why was this so? Perhaps it was because Rome, despite its many cosmopolitan features, was still a slave society at bottom. Its foundation, reflected in its slave system, was military and agricultural. Roman institutions were an extension of the family. From its slave-based farms and factories to its military and urban bureaucracies, the Greco-Roman civilization projected an ethos that was paternalistic, autocratic, and suspicious of new innovation.

As David Brion Davis,[6] the brilliant writer on Roman commercial culture notes, the youth growing up on a Roman farm saw a "human pecking order" constantly before his eyes, and its gradations of status, rights, and obligations based on age, gender, sex, occupation, and descent seemed as natural and inevitable to him as the changes of seasons.

Davis further suggests that Roman commerce was an extension of the Roman family. The civil service and business were familial in their methods of recruitment and promotion. A youth might be placed in business under an uncle or a cousin. In middle age, he would, in his turn, sponsor relatives or kinsmen. Even if he were engaged in an occupation or appointed to an office under a non-relative, the youth was still expected to behave as a surrogate son. He would show loyalty and respect for his employer, who, in turn, would keep an affectionate eye upon him, even aiding him in non-job-related affairs.

We who are accustomed to abstract principles would do well to recall that, for Cicero, wisdom is not an abstract system of declarative sentences from which particular conclusions can be drawn. Wisdom is always wisdom in a particular context—in his case, the Roman cultural tradition. Cicero's potentate is not an idealization of human virtue, but a player bound in a vast network of duties, obligations, and debts. Unlike Plato's sovereign, his advantages are only realized in reciprocal action. Plato's politics of redemption expresses unlimited aims and his rulers are unfettered by bonds forged through social exchange. Cicero's image of the cooperative, affiliative, collective goal-seeker is a necessary antithesis to the sophists' autonomous individual using the system for personal advantage. Similarly, Cicero's idea lacks the utopian sweep of Plato's rule by guardians, but is far more human and temperate.

The greatest practitioner of collective power in the ancient world was Augustus, who reigned as the first Roman Emperor (31 to 14 B.C.). His methods provided a model for ruthless Renaissance princes and the British rah. When Mark Antony and Cleopatra committed suicide after their defeat at the battle of Actium (32 B.C.), the victorious Octavius emerged as the unchallenged ruler of the entire Roman world. As the nephew of Caesar, Octavius enjoyed the loyalty of the army, but, in the chaos of the overthrow of the Republic, he faced a dilemma. The Senate, although it had failed Cicero utterly in his attempted restoration of the Republic and had thrown itself prostrate before the feet of the generals, still held a certain place in the hearts and minds of the Roman people. Despite its failures, it had been a part of the Roman system of checks and balances for centuries. The concept of dictatorship—however much the desperate Romans seemed willing to grant Octavius absolute power—was a temporary expedient for times of crisis.

To a lesser mind, all options for the future seemed blocked. Cicero's beloved Republic could not be restored. It had failed utterly; the apparatus of an overgrown city could not effectively govern a far-flung empire. On the other hand, Julius Caesar's military dictatorship had ended in assassination. Squatting in the ashes of a 500-year-old republican tradition, the Senate was unalterably opposed to one-man rule; yet, the belief was widespread that Rome could be saved only by concentrating power in the hands of a single individual. Augustus solved the contradictions by building a system that surrounded and encompassed all the previous ones.

The new system allowed Augustus to be both dictatorial and republican at the same time. He called himself princeps (which means first citizen), while exercising kingly powers. He restored the Senate, but permitted it to function with only a shadow of its old powers. Thus, while preserving all of the old republican trappings, he stripped the people who had exercised a measure of power under that system of their efficacy. He created new structures outside of the old forms. Rome was henceforth to be run by an emperor and his senior civil servants. He fulfilled Aristotle's formula for persuading the masses: "Use old wine in new bottles or new wine in old bottles."

What was the result? Under the imperial structure of Augustus, Rome created a peaceful and prosperous trading area that stretched from Scotland to India. During the next two centuries, when writers like Tacitus or Quintilianus looked back, they may have lamented the loss of republican eloquence and the lack of stormy controversy, but they recognized the new security and comfort as an almost unmitigated blessing. Although Rome finally lost its organizing mission, its memory haunted the world. The ideal of the universal state served as a model for Christendom, the League of Nations, the United Nations, and many dreams of world government.

Augustus harnassed the full propaganda resources of Rome to maintain his power. His image on coins kept his countenance constantly before his subjects everywhere in the Empire. Statues were erected from Gaul to Macedonia to the lands of the Berbers celebrating the triumphs of his reign and identifying him with the pantheon of gods. Rome's greatest writer, Vergil, writes of the inevitability of Roman triumph in the *Aeneid,* an epic in which Aeneus and his descendants sail from Troy to found Rome under divine favor. The lesson of the work is dramatically clear: it is futile to resist the Romans, a masterly people who are organizing the world under a mandate from the blessed gods.

The most decisive feature of the Roman power-state was the development of an educational system for the recruitment of a loyal and efficient civil service. This key stratum was crucial for Roman dominance. The Roman capital was more than just the primary polis of the empire. It was the nerve center of a great network — the home base for the civil service and the army. Established under Quintilianus (35-118), named the "Supreme Controller of Roman Youth," the educational system was built upon the foundation of the study of Rhetoric, the art of effective speaking and writing. Rhetoric codified the theory and practice of the great orators, statesmen, lawyers, and poets of the Ciceronian, Golden, and Silver ages, and, thus, became a verbal technology for the ruling class.

Instruction began very early; Quintilianus envisaged instruction beginning in the nursery. Four- and five-year-olds memorized maxims and fables, and later learned inspirational myths and stories from Roman history. Later, they assimilated the epics and heroic poetry. They were drilled in the techniques of dilating upon a question, expanding on an idea or motif, filling out a narrative theme, or pursuing a line of argument. Mock law courts produced readiness and fluency. The end products were steeped in traditional wisdom. They could speak or write on either side of an issue with equal facility. A common body of literary study provided a sense of membership in an educated class. The graduates formed a pool of officials and functionaries with a common language, literature, values, and skills. Their verbal and written skills were well-adapted to ruling over a vast panoply of subject peoples.

Renouncing Power: Doctrine of the Stoics

The Stoics called for a renunciation of power. Their anti-power doctrine was a survival formula for the autonomous cosmopolitan individual adrift on the vast human ocean of the Greco-Roman world. Developed by Zeno of Citium (Cyprus), Stoicism was a response to the death of the city-state as an independent entity. As the state ceased to be the focus of individual aspiration and the center of gravity for security, career opportunities, and religious feelings during the late Empire, ordinary people were cast adrift. With the authority of the state coming under a cloud, the individual turned inward to internal resources and outward to doctrines of universal significance. Renunciation of power formed the ethic of the world citizen. Elements of Stoicism strongly influenced both Christianity and Renaissance Humanism.

The Stoic transcended tribe, race, and city, celebrating the brotherhood of man and proclaiming that the true philosopher, as a citizen of the world, was at home everywhere. The origins of Stoicism are rooted in the decline of the autonomous polis. The empires of Philip of Macedon and his son, Alexander the Great, had undermined the independence of the city-states, removing their walls and turning them into mere tax-collecting points and sub-administrations. A citizen had found meaning, value, and significance in daily participation in the life of the polis. It was an arena for the realization of what the Greeks referred to as *arete*, or excellence, a place where the amateur lived a many-sided life, playing the role of athlete, actor, artist, statesman, merchant, and military officer within the span of a single life.

The new imperial order called for specialists to perform specific functions in a vast imperial network. The social space which had nurtured the multi-talented intellectual no longer existed. The Greek intellectuals of the Golden Age, such as Gorgias and Protagoras, had been founders of schools, entrepreneurs, ambassadors, state advisors, teachers, and free-lance philosophers. The old community, the city-state, had supported such many-sided geniuses, but it was gone. Empires did not need ambassadors but civil servants, not intellectuals but catalog makers, and, especially, they did not need teachers of rhetoric and political wisdom when the old forensic drama of the polis had disappeared. The multi-faceted Aristotle had been replaced by the librarians of Alexandria; Gorgias by tax collectors; and Plato by civil servants. In an Imperial setting, the intellectual no longer sought the goal of mastering all knowledge. Intellectuals became denatured, institutionalized, mere functionaries of the state.

The psychological withdrawal from the polis was filled by the majesty of the Empire, but a similar withdrawal took place in Roman times from the fourth century A.D. onward. Particularly in the western half of the Empire, population declined, the sources of slaves began to dry up, international trade in luxury goods was threatened by the return of pirates to the Mediterranean, and inflation increased eight-fold during the fourth century, despite the desperate measures of reform emperors. The boundaries of the Empire shrank and were consolidated in the face of barbarian pressure. The enormous Germanic birthrate spilled into Northern Italy, Spain, and Gaul, and the army became predominantly barbarian even unto its officer class. The Roman tax system was weakened by barbarian invasion, eroded by declining numbers and resources. Troubles over the succession of emperors, revolts in the military, declines in education and in civic services brought the authority of the state under a heavy pall. Affairs became so desperate that rich persons were punished by being enrolled as tax collectors (the state reasoned that the rich could make up deficiencies in revenue from their own pockets). Offices that had been high honors in the early Empire were now awarded as sentences for criminal acts.

During the fourth century, it had become clear that Rome could no longer solve its problems. Citizens were fleeing into the open countryside; slaves were becoming serfs under the protection of former Roman military officers; and people were physically and psychologically withdrawing from a state that could no longer provide career opportunities, essential civic services, or even basic security, and which had lost its power as a center for human aspiration. In the chaos of the breakup of Empire, a genius named Augustine of Hippo (354-430) found a new point of integration for human loyalty. He filled the vacuum left by the disintegration of the Western Empire with a new vision, an alternative consciousness, as it were.

Preacher, expounder of doctrine, and administrative expert, Augustine devised a plan that allowed Christianity to survive the destruction and abandonment of the old civic culture. He needed to separate the Christian way of life from the dying administrative machinery of Rome. From Emperor Constantine onward, emperors had tried to refurbish the empire by using Christianity as a focus of identity for its diverse and restless population. Thus, in the midst of decay, Christianity set about its task of unifying and revitalizing Rome. Despite the outcry of the old pagans, who still formed a majority, that it was precisely the Christian values of meekness, compassion, and love that had undermined the stern old Roman virtues of duty, sacrifice, and will, the new religion quickly became involved in problems of civic administration and imperial governance. By the time Augustine watched the Germans sack Ravenna in 410 A.D., the Church had become so tightly bound to Roman administration that many Christians feared that they were now shackled to a corpse.

As one group after another was being left to its own resources, Augustine developed a plan for people to survive the death of their cities. A new community, the monastery, became the model of a new era—a subsistence agriculture and handicrafts community. In order to use them as object lessons in settled habits, peaceful planning, and prosperous cooperation, he planted them in the very heart of the ferocious Germanic forestlands.

The psychological withdrawal from Caesar had to be filled with a psychological renewal and reintegration. A new vehicle for human participation had to be constructed. Augustine sought a form of power that rested on the participation of the organic community. Moral authority had to be demonstrated in the lives of individuals. To revivify a Church that had depended increasingly upon form and ritualized compliance since the time of Constantine, Augustine recommended that farmers, fisherfolk, and other proletarian diamonds-in-the-rough be proselyting ministers.

Augustine advised ministers to bind their members to the community in a new way. They were not merely to dispense religion to the faithful, but to treat them as active learners. According to Augustine, faith must be an achievement. The very difficulty of conversion becomes a powerful asset. Those who struggle the hardest are bound into the new creed most securely because of the severity of the rites of passage. The opacity of doctrine, the meagerness of some evidence, the labor of making interpretation, and the necessity of working through ambiguous signs and arcane symbols demand in-depth participation and make the ultimate enlightenment all the stronger. This journey was modeled on Augustine's own experience. He had struggled through a multiplicity of doubts, dissipations, rival creeds, and hard-won interpretations in order to achieve his conversion.

In his work *On Christian Doctrine*, Augustine reasons that, if God provided irrefutable occular proof, there would be no need for faith or, for that matter, any need for an institutional Church.[7] Likewise, there would not be any need for initiation, conversion or Church hierarchy. The long journey through doubt and the final leap of faith binds the believer into the Church in a way that a lucid and absolutely convincing demonstration never could. This rationalist tradition of an unfolding faith (conspicuously absent in the Byzantine and Russian traditions) which reveals itself in accord with the needs of each new age was never wholly lost. The role of Church leadership passed from defender to creator. In implementing the idea of the believer as learner and expositor, Augustine developed his famous "doctrine of signs"[8] as a method for the interpretation of Biblical stories and symbols.

In yet another area, Augustine was able to turn the dismal prospect of Rome's coming collapse into an occasion of joyous expectancy. Augustine's brilliantly simple and appealing view of human history is that of a progressive series of apocalyptic events culminating in a dramatic final judgment. He felt that his contemporaries should have greeted the end of the Roman world with happiness, not despair, for, although the city of man was decaying, the city of God[9] was near at hand. Augustine reminded his people that the Secular City was irretrievably flawed. Its founder had been Cain, a murderer and an exile. Sin was at its heart and was involved in the very act of its founding. Its dissolution was necessary. The end of Rome was a prelude to the end of historical time. Thus, Augustine's teaching promoted social cohesion and hope in the midst of the most terrible disasters.

The Middle Ages: Power as Invisible Order

During the Middle Ages (500 A.D. to 1400 A.D.), there was little concern about power and no significant formal speculation about its nature. From the fall of Rome to the rebirth of the western free-labor city, Europe was dominated by the ideals of otherworldly salvation.

After the seventh century, Europe was cut off from Africa and the Middle East by the Arab Conquests and pressed from the North and East by throngs of barbarians. Coinage and international commerce were gone, and the ruined, depopulated cities survived only because they served as centers for Church administration. Even the kings of the era began as semi-nomadic rules governing from encampments in the field.

The essentially medieval communities were three in number: they were the manor house, the monastery, and the peasant village. The manor house was the bulwark of feudalism, and the monastery preserved whatever remained of Greco-Roman learning outside the classical world. Of course, power was exercised by the local prince, the village priest, occasional dynastic rulers, and the heads of the great abbeys and religious houses. The Gallacian swords, the secular and spiritual authorities, received routine compliance.

The lot of the great bulk of the people was powerlessness. Ritual obedience was perceived to be the natural order of things. The ideal of the fully developed, assertive individual had died with the classical world and did not emerge again until the urban world arose in the Renaissance with its demands for daring virtuosity. In a collective, earth-rooted medieval society, no one dreamed of mounting an independent bid for power; Thomas Hobbes' restless, power-mad individual had not yet appeared. Power arrangements were sanctioned by the divine order and, as such, were invisible.

Power and Terror: The Concept of Machiavelli

The greatest power treatise of the Renaissance is that of Niccolo Machiavelli (1469-1527). *The Prince,* a manual for rulers who wish to gain and hold on to power, has been characterized as the first wholly secular treatise of the modern world. Living at a time of great disorder, when his beloved Italy was being dismembered by rival republics and menaced by France, Spain, and the larger German provinces, Machiavelli attempts in *The Prince* to provide a success formula for power politics. It has been claimed that Machiavelli's little book was an advertisement for his services addressed to aspiring Italian princes on the lookout for some ruthless and cunning political advisor. Nothing could be more absurd in light of Machiavelli's personal situation. First, his reputation was already in shreds.

Secondly, his work exposes the "secrets" in such a frank and brutal way that few princes would be willing to avail themselves of a used-up secretary who had given away the best of the family jewels.

Further, it is well to remember that the so-called self-styled princes that Machiavelli pretends to advise were not secure members of ancient hereditary houses. They were upstarts and adventurers who held their power precariously, as they lacked the authority of tradition, public affection, or high moral example.

It is not surprising, then, that Machiavelli draws a distinction between the demands of morality and the demands of successful politics. He declares that the Christian virtues of compassion, loyalty, and forebearance are no more applicable to the conduct of successful politics than they are to the conduct of a successful military campaign. A humanist scholar thoroughly acquainted with classical literature and accustomed to searching for solutions to contemporary (Renaissance) problems in ancient Greek and Roman sources, Machiavelli finds his justification in Livy. According to Livy, the virtues of one sphere of human endeavor may be incompatible with those of another. He argues that the virtues of the warrior would be montrously inappropriate for the peaceful conduct of civic affairs, but they are essential in their own sphere. Just so, for Machiavelli, the moral law exists and receives its due, but those who honor it will not be able to be effective in their use of power. The successful politician must make heavy compromises with Christian virtues. Similarly, the study of politics must not be shackled by the tenets of moral law. Just as law and medicine are independent disciplines and not branches of religious thought, politics must be studied on its own terms and not under the auspices of moral law.

Machiavelli proposes that the prince adopt the following guide in establishing and maintaining effective power:

1. **Terror as a Weapon:** The one in power should use violence sparingly, but promptly. It must be sudden and overwhelming. If the use of power is massive and merciless, he will have to use it but seldom. It is the fear caused by the credible threat of violence that is decisive in controlling the behavior of others. Terror should never be used in incremental stages (the ratchet theory), and threats should never be made, unless one is ready to carry them out.

2. **Set Your Enemies Against One Another:** The ruler will identify the most powerful members of his constituency and sow dissension among them. All those who are likely to challenge his position must always be at one another's throats. Similarly, he will foment trouble between rival princes to weaken and distract them.

3. **The Rule of Expediency:** "A prudent ruler does not have to keep faith when to do so would be to his disadvantage... If all men were good this would not be good advice, but as they are bad, won't keep their faith with you, it follows that you do not have to keep faith with them." Benito Mussolini was profoundly influenced by the writings of Machiavelli. The Second Secretary of Florence's works were often discussed in Mussolini's father's blacksmith shop. He seems to

have been particularly impressed by Machiavelli's teachings on expediency, and they are reflected in Il Duce's drafting of foreign treaties. He enjoyed the propaganda value of these "scraps of paper" which he had no intention of honoring.

4. **Be a Dissembler:** Again in *The Prince,* he writes: "But it is necessary to disguise one's conduct and to be a good actor and dissembler." He tells us that people notice the surfaces of things and not the depths. Outward appearance masks interior machination.

5. **Motives:** Human nature does not change; hence, the relevance of classical examples. People are moved by love, hate, and fear. The most powerful of these is fear. It is well to be loved, but love only moves a few, perhaps a little company of saints. On the other hand, "if your people hate you, all your fortresses won't save you," and hatred of the enemy cannot be sustained in the hearts of the people. Fear is best. Let your friends, enemies, and potential allies live in fear of you.

The Worship of Order

For Thomas Hobbes (1588-1667), in his work *Leviathan,* social order is the supreme justification for concentrated, centralized power. According to Hobbes, the best society is one in which absolute power is vested in a single individual. Whatever diminishes the power of the executive must be suppressed. The mechanism of countervailing power — parliaments, checks and balances, power-sharing agreements — must be smashed ruthlessly. Only a powerful monarch can guarantee the stability of the social order and the security of his subjects. In order to consolidate its power, the monarchy must gain control over the community's language, culture, and laws. Hobbes believes that these areas must be "geometrized" — made as regular, as lucid, and as predictable as geometry.

Like many persons obsessed with autocratic power, Hobbes was a fearful and insecure man. He was born in a time of terror, for reports of the Spanish Armada were filling England with alarm at the time of his birth on April 15, 1588. This event explained (so he maintained) his lifelong love of peace and security. This love was never to be gratified. He was often dependent on the whim of patrons, was savagely attacked by Roundheads and Cavaliers alike, and was finally forced into exile.

The young Hobbes distinguished himself as a classical scholar, completing a translation of Thucydides in 1628, the year of the Petition of Right and the dramatic beginning of the violent struggle between king and parliament. Thus, its publication in the stormy, star-crossed year of 1629 seemed peculiarly apt to Hobbes, who saw a warning against democracy in the defeat of ancient Athens.

At the age of forty, Hobbes, browsing in a gentleman's library, first looked into Euclid's *Geometry.* He is supposed to have cried out, "This cannot be so." In disbelief, he began to trace back the proofs through proposition after proposition. Struck with the "lawful beauties" of the system, he made its rigorous logic an ideal standard for all speech, thought, and conduct.

His struggle to attain first principles was further excited some years later when, at a learned gathering, he heard a voice ring out, "But, sirs, what is the fundament? Sirs, what is sense?" No one could answer. The question haunted Hobbes' dreams and days. Finally, he came to the conclusion that the causes of all things lay in what he called "the diversity of motion." To study motion became his obsession. Geometry would be his guide and method.

In 1632, Hobbes discussed the laws of motion with the aged Galileo, and any student of Hobbes' works will notice the influence of Galileo's clockwork vision as a kind of primitive social physics. In 1640, Hobbes went into exile in France having alienated Monarchists and Puritans alike.

In 1651, he wrote *Leviathan*, a book that is rigorously materialistic in its conception of power. The work extends the principle of motion from the natural sciences to the social sphere—a social physics. According to Hobbes, the essential element of animal and human behavior is found in two kinds of motion. The first kind of motion, Hobbes calls vital (blood, heartbeats, breathing, digestion) and the second, voluntary (the will). Motion that is aimed at attaining an object is called desire; motion in retreat is called aversion. The mainspring behind human motion is power.

Unfortunately, man's desire for power is limitless. Hobbes avers: "In the first place I put for a general inclination of all mankind a restless and perpetual desire for power after power, which ceaseth only in death."[11] The power of an individual is defined as the "present means to obtain some apparent future good."[12] Without a single individual who exercises firm control, the world will always be a war of each against all. His world, like Galileo's, is mechanistic. A world without the gravity of a central body is an arena of whirling collision. Much of public life in a democracy is a great cracking of sinews, of herculean engagements, of faction wasting its substance in a struggle against rival faction.

Hobbes supposes that the state had its origin in the search for order among exhausted combatants. Not from altruistic idealism or compassion for wounds suffered, but from a selfish desire to protect life and property, individuals contracted with the prince for their own protection. However, once having contracted with the prince, they were unable to break the agreement.

The Eighteenth Century: Doctrines of Limited Power

It is well to recall that the "Age of Reason" is a term with rather limited application. It may be applied to largely middle-class administrators who constructed the expansionist autocracies of the eighteenth century, and to the intellectual critics of monarchic and aristocratic privilege. For the masses, it was an age of passion. Dissenters wailing on Welsh hillsides, mobs crying out "No Popery!" in the Gordon Riots, opium-eaters in the new industrial cities, and farmers dying of cholera were not aware that the Goddess of Reason ruled Western Europe. It might as well have been called an age of fear. These new masses, cut adrift from the old rural medieval institutions that had given them identity, had been set in motion. Shorn of their religion, culture, and the village conventions of social control, they became the new goths disturbing the sleep of the old aristocracy and the new merchant class.

In the latter half of the eighteenth century, the rising middle classes began to fear another sort of passion. This was the passion of autocrats who abused their power and arbitrarily extracted the wealth of the nation for dynastic war. To prevent unchecked exercises of power, a new scheme of power allocation emerged—one that would scatter power among the various constituencies of the nation. The new idea of democracy, of locating power in the people, had unintended results. The citizen was now considered an active creator and participant in the national culture so that, as the state gained in legitimacy, it also grew in authority. Thus, out of fear of concentrated and arbitrary power was born the modern state with the authority to confiscate one-third to one-half of its citizens' incomes, to conscript its male citizens in huge numbers for defense, and to intervene in what used to be considered the private affairs of its people. The modern power state would have made an eighteenth century autocrat's head swim. His tiny professional armies, his crude methods of extracting wealth, and his colleges of officials were the toys of an amateur compared to the mobilized societies of the twentieth century that have brought us total war on civilian populations and the tribal *gesellschaft*.

The ideas of limited government, of sectors of leverage, and of a dialectic forensic test of ideas (as opposed to dynastic imperatives) became cultural obsessions in Europe and America. Two thinkers are of special importance here.

John Locke (1632-1704) developed the roots of the idea of limited sovereignty. According to Locke, limited governmental power is necessary to create the social and life space around the individual that is needed for freedom and happiness. Locke writes that when a government violates an individual's rights to life and liberty, it loses its legitimacy, and those who would ordinarily be the bulwarks of the government (those people who have either made it or do the most to sustain it) have the right to overthrow it. This idea was a basic belief for the leaders of the French and the American Revolutions. Jefferson's words of the Declaration bear a strong resemblance to those of Locke's Second Treatise.

Baron de Montesquieu (1689-1755) was a very discerning student of history and a harsh critic of political systems. Montesquieu implements

Locke's theory, giving it a program and a method. According to
Montesquieu, limited sovereignty can be realized by a separation of powers
and a system of checks and balances. In his system, the authority and
functions of government would be divided between King, lords, and
commons. This idea of limitation of power (the government as a balance of
forces) seemed peculiarly appropriate for the United States, then an infant
nation with a profound fear of arbitrary centralized power.

The Arrogance of Power: Edmund Burke

Enemy of the French Revolution, friend of Samuel Johnson and of the
American colonists, writer, philosopher, statesman, and literary critic,
Edmund Burke (1729-1794) had a deep aversion to intellectuals in power.
For Burke, every intellectual is a dangerous revolutionary. In imposing their
abstract visions of an ideal world upon others, intellectuals show little
regard for the loyalties and traditions of ordinary people. They generally
feel contempt for the commoners' hard-won beliefs and for the special
circumstances of their local communities. Burke feels that intellectuals in
power promptly set out to fix what is not broken, to demolish arrangements
that have been working for centuries, and to impose grand and sweeping
plans that are foreign to the experiences and beliefs of the people who are
forced to carry them out.

According to Burke, the intellectual's mania for novelty and taste for
utopian solutions were tragically realized in the failures of the French
Revolution. In the name of an abstract idea which not one of them could
define, they crippled the agricultural system, ruined foreign trade, and
confiscated huge masses of property. They outlawed the historic creed of
ninety-eight percent of the people and substituted a religion devised by
Robespierre. This new religion was hastily and clumsily imposed on the
masses by those at the top. To fill the vacuum left by the "removal" of
Christianity, the church of reason took over many of the old familiar
forms. It had its own feast days (the anniversary of the Fall of the Bastille,
the anniversary of the King's death, etc.) It had its own saints, the martyrs
of the revolution, and its own ceremonies, rituals and sacred books.

Of course, the new religion laid an egg. Before a massive crowd, sparks
from the burning statues of the enemies of Reason set fire to the statue of
the Goddess of Reason. The fire was put out, but not before the statue was
badly damaged. With Robespierre presiding as high priest, the new religion
had been made to look ridiculous before the masses; henceforth, he would
rely on terror.

Burke was appalled by what he felt were the excesses of the Revolution.
He traced these excesses to the beliefs of the Jacobin intellectuals who had
created the climate of ideas in which the Revolution had germinated.[13] Their

rejection of the past as a repository of wisdom had led them to a shallow faith in *a priori* ideas. Their belief in the basic goodness of human beings led them to attack ancient institutions as repositories of repression. Their belief in utopian moral progress led them to use the moral grandeur of an idea as an unassailable proof of its correctness. Their belief that past societies had been governed by arbitrary and irrational laws, coupled with an exaggerated assessment of the effectiveness of dedicated individual action, fed their tendency toward improvizational violence.

The intellectuals, such as Voltaire and Rousseau, kept up a steady drumfire of social criticism that did much to undermine the self-confidence of the old governing groups. It taught the ordinary French people to regard their government as irrational and exploitative. The nobility apologized for their privileges, while a corrosive rhetoric dominated the letters of the salon, newspaper, manifesto, novella, broadside, and popular ballad. The final blow came when the government suffered a massive financial crisis and power passed to the Jacobins.

The execution of the Royal family, the crushing of the nobility, the weakening of the old religion, the mobilization of the masses, and the hasty enactment of untried reforms appeared to Burke to be a grand lesson in the irresponsible use of power. What is a responsible use of power? Power must be exercised, but it must be exercised humbly and responsibly rather than arrogantly. Power, according to Burke, should be used only when prompted by specific grievances. Its mandate covers only the amelioration of concrete evils.

This conservative use of power is rooted in a conservative idea of society. In Burke's view, society is not a mechanism to be tinkered with, but a biological organism, a living creature. This theory, which came to be known as organicism in the next century, states that society is an organic whole with each part sustained by every other part. By contrast, one may easily and confidently replace the parts of a machine; one may even redesign the mechanism, transforming it utterly, and add new functions. When it wears out, one discards it without a pang. One does not, however, treat a living body like a machine. We do not routinely change, replace, or redesign parts— at least we were not able to do so in Burke's time.

To choose to think about society as a living creature suggests a far more reverent and cautious attitude toward it than to conceive of it as a machine. It follows that the past of any community is the long record of its growth, development, and learning and not a vast scrap heap of folly, error, and crime. Its institutions are the fruit of hard-won experience; its collective wisdom is immense. Thus, if institutions continue to function (even if sometimes poorly), they are not to be overthrown lightly. Surely, it is an act of arrogance to demolish a society and replace it with an untried scheme. Then, too, sometimes problems (like fevers) are merely symptoms of diseases; at other times, they may be even healthful, a necessary struggle by the body to heal itself. Probably some problems are better ignored. Activism is not always a virtue.

In addition, Burke does not place much stock in planning. The world is too complex for planning. A livable neighborhood, a prosperous city, and a great empire are the results of accidental circumstances and luck. The noblest objectives are overthrown by unforeseen contingencies. The clumsy and absurdly optimistic schemes of intellectuals and reformers often lead to chaos and misery.

Despite the fact that he has the reputation of a man who fought off revolution, there was one group of revolutionaries who received Burke's enthusiastic support. Burke strongly supports the cause of the American colonists in his famed "Conciliation With The Colonies"[14] address. Here Burke stresses that the Americans are a practical people fighting for concrete objectives. Unlike the utopian French intellectuals who fought for such abstractions as Liberty, Equality, and Fraternity, the Americans are concerned with practical matters like taxation, fishing rights, and tariffs. Their demands are limited to specific issues that can be redressed by finite pieces of legislation. Burke's arguments are drawn from the practical circumstances organic to each situation. Burke purports that it is unwise to fight the colonists because of the concrete factors involved (the long coastline, the size of the population, the destruction of the resource base, the length of supply lines, etc.) and not because of abstract moral principles or involved legal imperatives. He felt that Americans understood his practical reasoning, and he felt a hardheaded affection for them. Of course, if Burke had seen the declaration written less than 15 months later by a Virginia intellectual, Thomas Jefferson, he might have tempered his judgment of the American character a little. The Declaration is as utopian as a document can be, and the Constitution is abstract enough to please the most Jacobin intellectual.

American Attitudes about Power: Jefferson Versus Hamilton

American ambivalence about power is rooted in its traditions of individualism and in its revolutionary birth. The tension between state power and individual autonomy has been with us since the infancy of the republic.

The founders of the nation drew very different lessons about the legitimate exercise of power from the experience of nation-building. Throughout the long debates over the Articles of Confederation and the Constitution, their discussions turned upon a fundamental point: how much power should remain with the people and how much should be vested in the government? The revolutionary ideology that emerged framed a fundamental agreement about the locus of power:

1. All *legitimate power* is vested in the people; thus, every action of government is ultimately justified by a mandate from the people.
2. The principle of determining the will of the people is numerical (majority rule—later expressed as the utilitarian calculus or the greatest good for the greatest number).
3. The power of government is "loaned" or delegated to representatives and periodically returned to the people through the agency of an election.

The State as Dismasted Hulk: Thomas Jefferson

The most lyrical expression of the eighteenth century fear of centralized power was expressed in the thought of Thomas Jefferson (1743-1825). He sees the federal government as a protector rather than as a regulator and an enabler. He hopes that it will not harass the people or "waste their substance" and, in general, will interfere in the affairs of the people as little as possible. He feels that the government should not engage in grandiose and theoretical schemes. Power should remain with the people.

Issues should percolate up from the grass roots through local leaders. Only their final crystallization and implementation is the job of government. Further, the people are able to resolve most of their own affairs on a local level, and local government is important to them. The nearer the government and the greater its possibilities for citizen participation, the more jealously guarded will be its prerogatives. Thus, over against federal government, state, county and township governments retain significant powers.

This concept of decentralized and limited power is grounded in a vision of America as a nation of small- and middle-sized farmers. The farmer is considered the model citizen and worthy of special attention by the government. The independent yeoman is a landholder and a producer of wealth; thus, he has an automatic stake in the nation and its future. Stable and serious-minded, he also has those special virtues that come from close contact with the wonders of God's Creation. This doctrine, with roots as deep as Cicero, Horace, and Arcadian legend, was fortified by Anglo-Saxon literary nostalgia for the vanished Saxon yeoman. Taken up later by Virginia's country gentry, it developed all the features of the agrarian myth so beloved of twentieth century scholars. It has continued to exert an influence on attitudes and policies up to our own time.

As any student of eighteenth century history will recall, the Jeffersonian view of power is opposed by the Hamiltonian positive state idea. In the Hamiltonian conception, the state takes a decisive role in the development of commerce. Under a strong executive, it pursues economic policies that bind the regions together, and it assures its citizens that the nation is respected (if not feared) abroad. Although the Federalists, after creating most of the institutions of government, suffered from hardening of the arteries by 1800, their idea had its first real flowering in Henry Clay's American System in which North, South, East, and West were seen as sinews to be bound together by the tendons of canals, railways, and turnpike roads.

The Federalists, despite their preference for a strong state role in developing commerce and industry, and their urban constituencies of merchants and professionals, also believed in the agrarian myth and in the primacy and importance of the farmer. They agreed with Jefferson that manufacturing breeds anonymous and dangerous masses and that there is something servile about a nation of shopkeepers. Popular belief told them that Rhode Island was a hotbed of dissent because of its urban and mercantile character. Connecticut, on the other hand, was a model of probity and stability because it had no proper seacoast, and its colonial inhabitants were farmers. The Federalists, themselves, were landowners (frequently owning large estates), as well as professionals and merchants. They liked an atmosphere of stability and order.

Their preference for a strong government and a powerful executive was only relative, and their desire for masterful state action was undermined by their revolutionary past in opposing the "tyrant," King George. The government they invented is, after all, one of checks and balances, of divided functions and powers. Modern advocates of a power state, by way of contrast, criticize the divided structure of our government as producing a polity that is constipated, slow to react, and frequently at war with itself. They cannot, of course, deny the stability of a government that has survived three industrial revolutions, waves of mass migration, and constant innovation in every area of society.

The general and pervasive American suspicions about concentrated power assured that the differences between Jeffersonian and Hamiltonian views were matters of degree rather than kind. Neither side could fully reconcile classical concepts of citizenship with a powerful central government, nor could they imagine a nation entirely shorn from the social control and moral ethos of the village or rural community.

The late Leo Marx,[15] author of *The Machine and The Garden*, metaphorically schematizes America's journey as a train moving across a vast landscape. Receding in the far distance is an arcadian landscape of small farms, glades, and flowering hillsides. Ahead is the Hamiltonian future—a mass of glass-bubble skyscrapers, orbiting apartments, and urban heliports. Almost all of the riders of the train (representing America) are gathered on the large rear platform in an unhappy cluster, their eyes fixed on the receding farmscape—our Jeffersonian rural past.

The scene illustrates our divided soul and the ironies of our attitude toward power. We have rejected the local gods, the local community, and economic autonomy for the atomization of the abstract society, but our nostalgia for rural values bites deep. This nostalgia is for an idealized vision of rural virtue, but we have deserted the land for the cities to a degree so massive that rural America is essentially unpeopled. We have depopulated rural America, stripped the power from its local institutions, all for what Jefferson might have seen as the mere empty careerism of the cities. Occasionally, we have returned to recolonize the hinterlands with branches of international corporations. For decades, reformers sneered at the mores of the countryside as provincial bigotry, as they concentrated more and more power in the Statehouses and in Washington.

The suburban return to the countryside after World War II did not reverse the flow of power, but actually augmented the power of metropolitan areas. Once a dominant majority, farmers are now a mere remnant in all but two or three of the so-called farm states.

Jefferson, himself, realized the contradiction between his belief in decentralized power and the preservation of agrarian dominance. Even by the time of his death in 1825, he could see that the increase in manufacturing and the consolidation of population in the cities were destroying the primacy of the farmer. A strong central government would have been able to protect the dominance of the farmer, but Jefferson had advocated a weak one. The lesson: strength can only be maintained by strength. There is, however, more to the story than this. A world that is deeply committed to preserving the facade of Jeffersonianism and the reality of Hamiltonian power has only one way out, constant manipulation. The nature and effects of this pervasive manipulation have not always been popular topics of discussion.

Thomas Carlyle (1795-1881), in *Heroes and Hero Worship*, celebrates the galvanizing power of the world historical personality. He discusses the hero as divinity (pagan mythology), as poet (Dante and Shakespeare), as prophet (Muhammad), as priest (Luther and Knox), as man of letters (Johnson and Burns), and as king (Napoleon and Cromwell). To Carlyle, mid-nineteenth century Europe was becoming a continent of shopkeepers and crossing sweepers. Only the hero could rouse the energy of the masses and hurl them in the wake of great adventures so that they could live their lives swiftly and keenly. Carlyle lost his early Scottish Calvinist faith, but his ideas are a secular version of Calvinism. Instead of the elect, we are presented with the hero, one who has been granted a special destiny from the beginning and whose life is an emblem for the salvation of ordinary people. Carlyle's writing is tortured, repetitious, and abstract. His impact upon German thought was at least as great as his influence in the Anglo-Saxon world.

Carlyle had ideas that differed very much from the reformers of his time. He felt that most people were much happier under a system of rigid hierarchy. According to Carlyle, democracy is pretense, but even that pretense wears down the energies of ordinary people. The constant compromise of principle, of giving up and glossing over original objectives, is an enervating activity. The politics of the shop, of the hustings, and art result in generally petty and exhausting exercises. Carlyle never believed friends who told him they loved to work closely with other people. He suspected most hated the compromise of ideals and goals and were merely uttering conventional pieties. Democracy, according to Carlyle, is just a new scheme for getting people to do as they are told, and it is one that renders them petty, tired, and disillusioned. Instead, people yearn to be led. They want to enlist under the banner of the exceptional leader and march out to the world adventure.

Decentralized Power

Adam Smith (1723-1790), author of *Wealth of Nations*, has two goals in this much-quoted work: to find natural laws and to contribute to the progress and happiness of society. Since work is the basis of all wealth, he argues for the worker's unrestricted right to sell his own labor; thus, Smith is a proponent of increasing the aggregate power of the people in a society, but an opponent of the increasing power of the government in society.

Smith thinks state coercion unnecessary.[16] For Smith, the job of intervention, regulation, and protection of individuals in the economic marketplace does not belong to the state and cannot be used as an excuse to augment its power. The invisible hand of free market competition is sufficient. Competition is the regulatory principle that prevents the people from being crushed by monopoly and coerced by rapacious officialdom.

Competition is a nearly unalloyed good. It is the inner dynamic of capitalism, the solvent of power, and the bulwark of freedom. Coercive economic power depends upon a monopoly of resources and effective control of consumer alternatives. Competition threatens monopoly and provides new alternatives; thus, it frees one from the power of others.

Market interference by the state must be restricted to a bare minimum, but Smith did not believe that the night-watchman state left us face-to-face with the claw and fang competition of the jungle. The discipline of the marketplace comes from the culture, not the state. Norms of fairness peculiar to the community continue to operate and to provide the moral climate in which all economic activity is situated. The rewards and sanctions of the culture are the backdrop of every business transaction. Competition does not take place within a vacuum. It is the activity of men and women who grew up in a particular place, were nurtured in a particular idiom of do's and do not's, must's and must not's.

The motif of state vs. culture is not taken to its logical extreme in Smith's work. There is a role for the state, albeit a negative one. This is evident in Smith's concept of economic justice. First of all, capitalism lacks a principle of regulative justice because, ideally, the distribution of goods and services is the result of thousands of individual decisions. The market system can thus operate without a societal consensus on the nature of justice. The state's role is reduced to a small, but potentially vital, one. Justice must be maintained by the removal of any artificial barriers in the way of equality of opportunity. A cynic might argue that this is the morality of system mechanics.

It is easy to fault writers for not anticipating the future. Smith was emphatically a man of his time, a clear-headed thinker of the Scottish Athens. He could neither have envisioned the enormous consolidation that destroyed parts of the free market, nor foreseen the rise of broadcasting and marketing or the power of their offspring advertising, a medium dedicated to persuading customers that there are no realistic alternatives to the purchase of certain products.

The Modern Power State: George William Hegel (1770-1831)

The German philosopher Hegel created a justification for unlimited power and a mandate for the leader, the so-called world historical personality. Despite Hegel's worship of reason and enlightened governance, his doctrines (and their mutations) have been used to sanction the most brutal and repressive acts.

Hegel's influence has been enormous, and most of us are Hegelians to one degree or another. It was Hegel who first interested us in the institutional history of mankind. Because of Hegel's massive influence, we have histories of trade, histories of fashion, and histories of military thought. Likewise, because of Hegel, we think in terms of national character, cultural epochs, historical mind sets, and style notes. We are no longer satisfied with the histories of battles and kings or with mere chronologies of events.

According to Hegel, history is not a random stream of events; it is an unfolding process that is both whole and meaningful. This unfolding is governed by a principle of rational necessity. The rational spirit is progressive. We cannot predict its future course, but, through the study of history, we can trace its successive material realizations as it mounts ever higher, moving from the neolithic mud to the starry heavens.

Where is the highest revelation of the world spirit of reason? Hegel found it in the autocratic Prussian state of his day. Since he violently rejected the idea that the rigid Prussian state could be improved, his philosophy became an ideological bulwark of militarists and reactionaries. Hegel made it clear that, as the course of the world spirit stood supreme over all individuals, the state transcended all individuals and their so-called rights.

Hegel's doctrine became a justifying philosophy for the autocratic leader as well. Napoleon's most opportunistic and ill-considered acts were seen as inevitable and historically necessary realizations of the world spirit in human form. Napoleon was the agent of reason on horseback. In a Germany that had been wounded and dismembered by Napoleon, the little corporal became a greater object of worship than in France. In awakening their national consciousness, he revealed himself to be an agent of history and the world historical personality before which everything must give way.

This hero cult of German philosophy had some dismal consequences. Instead of examining the causes of leadership or the kinds of conditions and constituencies that called it forth, it deified leadership as a mystical entity unto itself. Thus, leadership became a principle to be worshipped rather than a relationship to be carefully scrutinized as to its origins, functions, and consequences.

Smitten by Napoleon's success, Hegel, as high priest in the cult of history, also endorsed the principle of struggle as the agent of progress. By this standard, the happy nation was really a nation without history. Peaceful eras were blank pages of human history. Living in an era of tremendous upheaval on the one hand and autocratic heroes on the other, Hegel prostrated himself before the "judgment" of history and came close to affirming "that whatever happens is for the best" and "that which is, is right."

The Disillusionment: Schopenhauer Renounces Power

Arthur Schopenhauer (1788-1860) turned Hegel on his head. Schopenhauer taught that the center of things is not reason, as Hegel believed, but blind desire, itch, urge, or will. Reality is not the progressive triumph of the principle of reason, said Schopenhauer, but the consequence of a brute assertion of will. History is the product of the tragic violence and frustration of the will. The hungry will-force lay at the base. Its drive for power is unstoppable; like Ahab, it will strike the sun from the heavens if offended, and, in a fit of pique, it may someday rip the galaxy from its moorings. Its endless and joyless search for power is a guarantee of limitless suffering, broken worlds, and blasted hopes.

Arthur Schopenhauer lived for forty years in the same upper-class house in Frankfurt-on-the-Main, eating rich cuisine and drinking spirited, young wines, while he wrote the beauty of renunciation. The idol of the age, Bonaparte, the man of destiny on horseback, was a posturing, beady-eyed bandit. Caesar had been a bully, Alexander a conflagration rather than a man, and Louis XIV a monster of self.

Schopenhauer hoped the oriental doctrine of renunciation would sweep across the West, transforming the civilization of the saints and the scientists, but, looking to the future, he could already make out the shape of horrors to come. He foresaw a sacred national mission that would end in arson, rapine, pillage, murder, and robbery. He foresaw leaders who would never be satisfied until they burned Europe, devoured Asia, subjugated North America, and put South America and Australia on rollers.

Perhaps, just perhaps, Schopenhauer held, there is a role for reason after all. Surely, it can function as a corrective by pointing out the tragedy of human life, and it may show forth the necessity of putting an end to that life by murdering the will. "Renounce and stultify!" cried Schopenhauer.

Until the end of World War II, Hegelian thought was dominant in Germany, Europe, and much of the world. What a sea-change we have suffered. Since then, Arthur Schopenhauer's philosophy of death has crushed Hegel's pathetic faith in human reason.

The Power of the Masses

From the middle of the nineteenth century onward, the spectre of the masses haunted Europe. The fear of the potential power of the new urban masses, people uprooted by the millions to work in the mushrooming industrial cities, had been growing ever since the French Revolution. The belief that demagogs, half-educated street orators, and cynical adventurers would organize these discontented millions for mischief was not entirely baseless. The Paris Commune and the worker uprisings in Germany were merely harbingers of the huge mobilizations of the twentieth century. We should not forget that both fascist and communist organizers engaged in a battle for the streets in several European nations and that their very first objective was to reach the masses.

How did the masses come to be? Who were they, and how did they differ from the citizen? In a sense, the masses have always been present — in ancient Rome, we find a disinherited rural proletariat, shorn of their cultural traditions through mass migration, atomized, lonely and discontented. In another sense, however, the masses are a unique product of the nineteenth century and of the Industrial Revolution, when many European cities doubled or trebled their populations in a single decade, as they drained the countryside of hands for factory labor. In London, Paris, Berlin, Amsterdam, Munich, and Glasgow, hundreds of thousands of displaced rural migrants lived in squalor. In their rural communities, they had been poor, often propertyless, but they had not lacked a sense of identity. They had been members of a parish or of a guild. They belonged to large, extended families and were participants in a village cooperative or association. In the cities, they were shorn of these associations; they proved to be no more than atoms in a sea of strangers with other atoms who had been cut off from their past and from the rituals, mores, and constraints of the village. Intellectuals and administrators feared that someone would fill this loss of culture by providing a new and dangerous identity.

Nineteenth century intellectuals contrasted the masses with the citizen. The citizen, in its idealized form, is a potent concept. It is said that Rome fell, not because it could not solve its problems, but because it did not have enough citizens. The Greek city-state fell to the Macedonian conquerors because its people abandoned the citizen ideal. The citizen is said to be an individual with a sense of obligation to the larger community and pride in its achievements. He participates in its rites and governing procedures and equates the public welfare with his personal interests.

Romantic artists and writers blamed the existence of the detribalized masses on the greed of the new lords of the machine who had lured them to their dark, Satanic mills. The bourgeoisie struck back by blaming the intellectuals for calling all existing social and political arrangements into question. As a result, the disenchantment of the masses added to their vertigo and loneliness. After the revolutions of 1848, the question remained smouldering like a fire deep within the bowels of a ship: will these new populations of white savages, who have nothing to sell but their labor, be the new barbarians within the gates of civilization?

Gustave Le Bon (1841-1931), in his study *The Crowd*,[18] examines the behavior of urban collectivities in France and Germany. He is much interested in the bonds between the crowds, mere aggregates that appear to have nothing in common, and the street orators, radical leaders who forge the mass of disparate individuals into an active and serviceable weapon. Le Bon discovers two categories of leaders. The first group is that of the agitators. They display a sort of intermittent power of will that allows them temporary dominion over a crowd. They are audacious but weak, and, having collected the crowd, are unable to direct it beyond the gaining of a single objective. They may overrun a guard post or engage a body of police in an urban riot, but they are incapable of disciplining and organizing people for a protracted struggle. The second category consists of leaders with indomitable will who are much rarer, but whose work is far more enduring. These are "the true founders of religions and great undertakings."

> Whether they be intelligent or narrow-minded is of no importance; the world belongs to them. The persistent will-force they possess is an immensely rare and immensely powerful faculty to which everything yields. What a strong and continuous will is capable of is not always properly appreciated. Nothing resists it: neither nature, gods, nor man.[19]

Le Bon's meetings with street agitators both excited and depressed him. In his opinion, they were men of slight intellectual attainments but obsessed with a single idea which had taken hold of their lives. Deeply learned in their own monomania and armed with a single-minded passion, these men gave direction to crowds that were hungry to be directed by a masterful will.

Le Bon's conception of the city crowd is in line with the bogeyman conception of the masses that dominated the thought of his time. It was generally held that a collectivity of people becomes less intelligent than the least of its members; its intelligence is levelled down to that of a Pavlovian dog. On the other hand, all of its emotions are magnified; it is both suggestible and passionate. Finally, its sense of morality disappears as it hands over its conscience to its leadership. Because of its numbers, its sense of physical power is increased. These characteristics account for the crowd's extraordinary subservience to its leaders, its wild swings between cowardess and courage, its ability to slaughter, burn, and murder—acts that hardly a single one of its members would tolerate if acting alone.

The leaders insinuated themselves upon crowds through a process of affirmation, repetition, and contagion; thus, the crowd is acted upon by suggestion rather than reason. Indeed, Le Bon's study affirms that the majority of crowd members possess few clear-reasoned ideas on any subject whatsoever, outside of their specialty. His discussion of the process of communication between the leader and the crowd is not much different from Hitler's estimate of the masses in *Mein Kampf:*

> Affirmation pure and simple, kept free of all reasoning and all proof is one of the surest means of making an idea enter the minds of crowds. The conciser the affirmation, the more destitute the appearance of proof and demonstration, the more weight it carries. The religious books and legal codes of all ages have always resorted to simple affirmation. Statesmen called upon to defend a political cause and commercial men pushing the sale of their products by means of advertising are acquainted with the value of affirmation.[20]

Power and Social Class: Karl Marx

For Karl Marx (1818-1883), the struggle for power between classes is the central fact of history. The evolutionary progress of society is determined by the results of these struggles. Religious wars, strikes, revolts, and other "class" wars are the decisive events that drive society from lower to higher stages of development.

Today, our image of Marx is distorted by the hordes of nickel-and-dime revolutionaries who simplified and sloganized his message.[21] It is wrong to think of firebrand intellectuals fomenting violent revolutions and shaping history to their ideals. According to Marx, one cannot alter the process of history—at best, one can understand and "work" with it by casting one's lot with its emerging forces. Thus, Marx left his class and proclaimed solidarity with the proletariat on the grounds that they were the emerging agents of change. He was joining the side of the winners.

The triumph of the working classes is not an occasion for moral indignation or revolutionary zeal either. One does not really wish for the triumph of either side; all sides would finally be liquidated or transformed in the struggle. The process itself is an agent of history and cannot be avoided. In the final analysis, one's wishes do not really matter.

Ordinary people have a stake in the great struggles of history through their class membership. According to Marx, class identity is determined by one's relationship to the means of production. Some classes own or have access to the wealth-producing apparatus of the society; hence, they are dominant. Others have neither land nor resources, neither machines nor capital. They have only their labor to sell to the controllers of the means of production who might or might not purchase it, depending upon its scarcity or upon some marketplace advantage. Physically subordinate classes are also culturally subordinate, for their economic position determines their life chances, world view, belief system, and mores.

In Marx's day, the dominant bourgeoisie were factory owners, speculators, and great merchants—the high bourgeoisie. The masses were the proletariat, reduced to machine tenders who were deeply alienated from the production process and from the products of their own labor. In the middle, the petit bourgeoisie was caught between the great grinding stones of the two warring classes. Ultimately, according to Marx, they would be crushed by the high bourgeoisie and fall into the ranks of the workers.

For Marx, the economic realities of the society also dictate the division of labor. By the mid-nineteenth century, the division of labor in Western Europe had become so elaborate that workers no longer dealt with a total product, but with only a fraction of the production process. The craftsman's pride had been liquidated and a worker's control over the appearance, quality, and distribution of his product had been smashed utterly. Thus, the worker's only remaining bond with his work is economic. His bond with his employer has been shorn of social or familial considerations; he lacks identification with his craft; he is alienated from the products of his own hands.

Why does the worker not rise up and take hold of his own destiny? Marx maintains that he could not, because he is controlled by the dominant belief system, an ideology which both reflects and propagandizes the existing economic arrangements. The great weapon of the master class is its ideology, a rhetoric which penetrates every aspect of the society, justifying the authority structure and presenting the dominance of the bourgeoisie as morally correct and universally beneficial. Dominating the newspapers, educational system, and other channels of communication, the master class presents its arbitrary, self-serving, and incomplete view of the world as the only game in town. Its values are presented as universally applicable; its voice is the only voice.

Thus, the role of the Marxist intellectual is that of critic and rhetorician. Using Marxist dialectic, he raises the workers' consciousness of their place in history. He refutes the ideology of the master class by exposing their partisan greed beneath the eulogistic cover of their words. Like a tribune of the people, like an investigative reporter, he exposes the partisan class motivation under their idealistic appeals for free competition, their championing of the impersonal logic of the marketplace, and their tidy explanations of supply and demand.

In informing the workers, the intellectuals must not shrink from the consequences of their ideas. Marx hated reformers who nickel-and-dimed their constituencies with gradualism. He thought of compromise as a disguised attempt on the part of the ruling class to deflect the energies of the underclass into ineffectual and relatively harmless routines. By institutionalizing a problem with a bureau or commission, they take it out of public discussion, crush the leaders of the opposition in a welter of administrative busy work, and give to all the world the illusion that the problem is well on its way to being solved.

Similarly, the intellectual must not simplify doctrine for an immediate advantage in tactics. Late in life, both Marx and Engels complained about followers who simplified and rounded off their doctrines — turning them into slogans and stereotypical formulas for the action program of a revolutionary group. As students of revolution know, this is the fate of every doctrine that becomes a mass program. Its complexities and contradictions paralyze action and confuse the faithful. It is quickly edited down into a set of formulas that can be applied to any and all situations, and its leading ideas are transmuted into dramatic slogans and symbols to create a rapid, shorthand identification among the faithful. Of course, to reach the masses, he must be an interpreter of Marx; he or she must edit Marx to win over the faithful. The authentic, textual Marx is a confused, verbose, and ponderous author, as students who have waded through his six hundred-plus page *German Ideology*[22] (1846) will attest.

The Power of Religious Experience: Josiah Royce (1855-1916)

Together with William James, author of *The Nature and Variety of Religious Experience*, Royce was the foremost American student of the power of religious experience as a communal force. Raised in the raw frontier conditions of Nevada County, California, the young Royce was marked by the hunger of an unsettled people for peace and social order. A weak esthete, he escaped to the East and Harvard, where he became one of its monumental figures. Throwing off his slack, non-conformist beginnings, he became obsessed with religious faith as the most powerful element in human community. As the binding force of society, religious faith struck him as the source of human solidarity and civilized conduct. Royce theorized that religion socializes people in the values of loyalty, duty, and affection — the primary virtues that make an extra-familial basis of association possible.

Fascist Power: Modern Tribalism

Fascism as the dominant form of power has taken hold in many nations through its false promise of escape from modern angst. It offers each people a primitive blood bond, a tribal identity to replace the loneliness and atomization of the modern world. The community it offers is barbarism. The blood bond is a cruel hoax; yet, it has seduced millions. In the nineteenth and twentieth centuries, Facism attempted to lead individualistic, heterogeneous modern Europeans back to a seamless tribal web, the forest hordes of prehistoric consciousness. It exacted an enormous price from every nation in which it took root.

This regression to primitivism triumphed in Germany and Italy only through the liquidation of much cultural richness and human diversity. Fascist art was a pathetic parody of the Roman tradition. True Italian artists fled the country or went underground in Mussolini's Italy. German culture suffered an even greater butchery. Between 1880 and 1940, the thought of German-speaking lands dominated the world, producing Nietzsche, Schopenhauer, Freud, Jung, Heidegger, Tillich, and a host of others. From 1940 onward, its voice has been nearly silent in the concert of nations. Only in the past decade does it seem to have recovered a serious role in the intellectual life of the West.

Why did Fascism take hold in Germany? How could the land of the giants of music, of the most spiritual theologians and metaphysicians have embraced such an utter repudiation of Europe's high culture? Surely, a part of the answer lies in the desperation and moral bankruptcy of the times. The ordinary, common-sense life of the people no longer worked; communal bonds had been slashed to ribbons. The nation, having been defeated in war, shaken by revolution, deprived of valuable industrial regions in the West, and crushed by war debts, faced the future under grave handicaps. Its government had used inflation as a deliberate party policy for repaying the country's war debts and for financing imported raw materials for German factories. This false prosperity allowed it to meet scheduled payments and absorb millions of soldiers returning from the Great War. After a sunburst of brief success, the policy debauched the currency, destroyed private property, made savings worthless, and drove investment abroad.

The most alarming consequence was the destruction of the German middle class. This core element of all advanced nations can only exist when property is secure and currency is reasonably stable. Mass unemployment, industrial collapse, and national humiliation had destroyed the German people's faith in itself and in its leaders. In addition, the steady erosion of German religious belief and spiritual life that had been taking place for more than a century left a deep void that remained unfulfilled once the gods of secular materialism had failed.

Furious resentment remained a living force with the Versailles Treaty's frontier stipulations, war guilt clauses and reparations. Political disorders were a constant feature of the national life. Crazed war youths, unable to demobilize and aided by officers of the Army clique, staged the 1920 "Kapp Putsch" and, in 1923, the "Bierhall Putsch." Forces of the Left sought the fall of the new democratic government through the weapon of the general strike. The world-wide depression of 1929 was the final hammer blow. Thereafter, fanaticism triumphed.

Many have compared the Germany of the 1920's and the early 1930's to a gravely ill patient. Kenneth Burke, in his brilliant and prophetic "Rhetoric of Hitler's Battle," saw Hitler as a "medicine man" engaged in demonic healing rites.[23]

A. Hitler's (1889-1945) concept of power through tribalization is largely contained in the pages of *Mein Kampf*, a book written while Hitler was serving a five-year sentence (reduced to eight months) for the Bierhall Putsch. The full text is eight hundred pages long. It is turgid, disorganized, and full of clumsy sentences. Churchill, in a moment of self-parody, is supposed to have said of it: "Never in the field of human letters has so bad a book been sold to so many, and read by so few." Nonetheless, as a British newspaper publisher observed at the time, the parts dealing with mass persuasion are filled with insight. The book was written, in part, as a reaction to Hitler's grotesquely amateurish attempt to take over the government in 1923. The document reflects Hitler's capacity to learn from tactical mistakes and to sketch a demonic blueprint for the future.[24] For those who feel the book was a clear warning, it should be noted that nothing is said about death camps, gas chambers, slave labor, or many of the other horrors. In *Mein Kampf*, Hitler comes to the conclusion that he made several serious mistakes: he struck before he had enough resources behind the movement; the movement needed a facade of respectability—in order to get the money and backing he needed, the movement must shed some of its outlaw image; this time, when he took power, it must be perfectly legal.

Hitler's conviction about respectability will come as a surprise to those who hold a diabolical, Hollywood image of the Nazis. The horror of the Nazis (as Erich Maria Remarch attempted to tell us in 1941) was not that they were bizarre monsters, but that they were not. They were ordinary human beings who often committed monstrous acts within a framework of nine-to-five respectability. Hitler held the middle class and their virtues in contempt. He believed they would do almost anything if it were masked with the trappings of normality and conventionality; thus, the most depraved and brutal acts were carried out in clean rooms by well-groomed, orderly people with ledgers, clipboards, and modulated voices. Hitler's shock troops formed a genuine political party with all the pretenses of negotiation, parliamentary maneuvering, and coalition.

Hitler's theory of taking power is not a coherent body of doctrine, but appears throughout his writings and speeches as a kind of laundry list of ideas:

1. All power movements must begin with the masses. Hitler did not have any patience with the idea of building up a dedicated core of intellectuals or a secret core of fighters. The presence of the masses provided visible proof of a movement's power. Further, anything that interfered with direct communication with the masses must be stripped away.

2. Ideas must be simple, dramatic (preferably in slogan form), and they must be repeated endlessly. Hitler believed that the masses have no capacity for political thought, that their reasoning powers are very feeble, and that they generally have little faith in their ability to make thoughtful decisions. Thus, the party leader or leaders must articulate a very small stock of dramatic, vivid, and starkly simple ideas. Unlike intellectuals, the masses have no desire for novelty and complexity in political life; "therefore, the basic ideas must be turned into slogans (because these are catch phrases that are memorable and vivid), and they must be constantly repeated until they penetrate the public consciousness through a series of hammer blows.

3. The leader should have neither loyalty nor binding attachments. Ruthlessness allows him the element of surprise. It also allows him to make decisions entirely on grounds of efficiency, expediency, and technical merit without having to worry about the feelings of others or the human consequences.

4. One must involve youth and give it a central place. We forget that the most anti-human movements of the modern era were youth movements and not those of diabolical old men. The exuberance of youth is its capacity for fanaticism, which Hitler cynically exploited.

5. Never apologize; never admit you were wrong. When something must be changed, it must be removed from sight, and no admission of its former existence can be permitted.

6. Everything must be expressed in terms of absolutes. If one discusses two sides of an issue, the masses take it for weakness and indecision. "Perhaps on the one hand, but maybe to some extent on the other hand—but perhaps again the truth lies in between" is the language of temporizing professors. The leader must never admit to any modification or concede that the ideas of an opponent have any merit. Only passionate and dogmatic assertion will be seen as commitment on the part of the masses.

7. The leader's oratory must be passionate. Only passion will arouse an answering passion in the masses. The masses do not respond to abstruse ideas or elegant expositions, but to the stormy fanaticism of the orator.

8. The relationship between the leader and the masses is an intensely sexual one. Hitler spoke of "the male orator" wooing the

"feminine masses." He spoke of his speeches as if they were acts of seduction; the speech is the seed that the orator sprays upon the masses to impregnate them with his ideas. Indeed, observers of Hitler at rallies noted that he seemed to stiffen like a fire hose as the words gushed from him. The state of the audience varied from nausea to exaltation to insane excitement.

9. The masses in a secular society are bankrupt, and they hunger for faith. Hitler's doctrine was a demonic version of Christianity. It used all the basic categories that were familiar to a post-Christian people. It has often been pointed out that Hitler occupied the role of savior and prophet, and Munich was the sacred city (the Rome of the Reich); that the devil appeared in the guise of bolsheviks, Jews, French, or whoever happened to be handy, as long as there was only one devil at a time to concentrate all the hatred of the people upon and to serve as a complete explanation for all the regime's failures at the moment.

10. The ability to explain the world in mythological terms. Hitler used basic human patterns of experience (conflict with implacable enemies, suffering, betrayal, salvation, purification, vindication) to give meaning and structure to contemporary events. Furthermore, he had the gift of presenting his ideas in extraordinarily vivid and imagistic terms.

11. The creation of a scapegoat. In time of utter national exhaustion and bankruptcy, Hitler lifted the failures of the German people from their own backs and placed them upon others. In Hitler's mythology, these bankrupts could identify with the little street orator who had also suffered humiliation, but, like the superman of German legend, had been betrayed and misunderstood by the people. The scapegoat (often Jews, sometimes Bolsheviks or French) served as a total explanation for German failures. The scapegoat was blamed for everything — decadence in the arts, pornography, crime, broken families, unemployment, etc. Hitler blamed Jews for both Communism and Capitalism, inventing the lurid story of the Jewish factory owner and the Jewish labor agitator who turned out to be brothers. After hours, they met behind the factory to shake hands on their clever manipulation of the people on behalf of a vastly larger world conspiracy.

12. The use of all the resources of communication — drama, movies, searchlights, marches, and the vast choreography of the masses.

13. A mixture of idealism and crude material reward. Hitler believed that the masses would only act if they were goaded by a vision of idealism that would last beyond their own lifespans, but they would only continue to be entranced by it if they were given concrete periodic rewards along the way.

One of Hitler's favorite phrases was "sacred wrath." He believed that groups are not forged and held together by love, but by hate. Indeed,

Hitler's appeals are a sort of counterpoint to Gandhi's. His deepest belief about groups was that they are activated by fear, threats, and negative appeals. He, himself, attempted to motivate Germans by constantly telling them that their way of life was threatened and that they were about to be destroyed as a people if they did not act. He constantly repeated dire warnings about the future of their children. Hitler's refrain was constantly one of loss: unless you act, everything will be taken away from you. Others will take your land, wealth, and fragile prosperity; your children will be servants of others; your culture and values will be mocked; and those who once feared and respected you will humiliate you.

One final note about tribalism. The so-called love of the tribe is matched by frightful hatred of those outside the tribe. It is like a giant air conditioner. It blows hot one way and cold the other. Teutonic Germany had large Slavic minorities, as well as Hebraic and Latin pockets. Its Danish and Dutch minorities could be assimilated as a part of the tribe. The others were locked out of the tribal web; they could enjoy no rights that a "German" was bound to expect, despite the difficulty of reverting to German tribalism in a nation that was actually less Germanic in blood than Denmark, Sweden, Norway, and even polyglot England and Scotland.

Max Weber: Power and Leadership

Max Weber (1864-1920) is best known for his thesis relating Protestantism to Capitalism, but he was also an outstanding power theorist. He defined power as "the possibility of imposing one's will on the behavior of other persons."[25]

Despite this individualistic definition, Weber explores group and collective power in many of his works.[26] He develops the idea of "charismatic leadership" as a factor in the founding of religious organizations. He extends his study of leadership by examining modern bureaucracy as a "routinization of charisma," and he isolates the factor of "rationality" as a key element in the Western drive for power. Finally, he develops the notion of a key stratum of a population being given a license for power during times of rapid social change.

Born in 1864 in Erfurt, Germany, Weber was the eldest son of a liberal politician and the grandson of a wealthy linen manufacturer. His mother, Helena Weber, was a strict Calvinist. Her puritanical disapproval of her husband's daily round of social lionizing created great tension in the home. Young Max had an explosive temperament, which may have had its origin in the stormy domestic scenes of the Weber household. Except for military duty, Weber lived twenty-six of his first thirty years at home.

From the very first, he was an academic winner. His rise as a professor was meteoric. In 1894, Weber received an appointment at Berlin; in 1895, a professorship at Freiburg; in 1895, and in 1896, he was called to Heidelberg. He achieved national recognition in a single stroke. In 1895, he gave an electrifying lecture on German destiny as an Inaugural Address at the University of Freiburg. Weber's studies of the agricultural policies of Ancient Rome led him to examine the agricultural policies of contemporary Germany. His address struck savagely at the agricultural policies of the Junker Aristocracy. Although the entire nation (and Bismarck) paid deference to this group, its agricultural policies were economically backward and demographically destructive. Their dreary succession of potatoes and cabbages represented a resource in time of war; in times of peace, they represented a poor use of land and labor. Further, the Junkers encouraged German peasants to migrate to the Prussian cities and the rapidly industrializing West. Slavs were replacing German peasants in the eastern provinces of Prussia, and the area was ceasing to be ethnically German. After centuries of a Teutonic march to the East, Germans viewed this reversal as social dynamite. Weber was hailed as a prophet.

His greatest work *The Protestant Ethic and the Spirit of Capitalism* (1905) provides important insights into the relationship between ideology and social behavior. Weber asserts that the development of capitalism among the Calvinistic elements of Holland, England, Scotland, Switzerland, and, to a lesser extent, among the Huguenots of France and Pietistic elements of Northern Germany was the result of the accidental psychological consequences of Calvinism. Protestantism freed the special calling of the monk and nun from its institutional setting, and made this otherworldly aestheticism available to ordinary men and women. The secularization of the monastic calling produced the early capitalist heroes who postponed gratification beyond their own lifetimes (it often took twenty-five years for a trading argosy to Asia to pay off) and worked out their secular salvation. The badge of this salvation was worldly wealth. Despite the popularity of this thesis, Weber lived to see it challenged. The Protestant ethic itself was savagely attacked by Wunderkind Stefan George, Leo Tolstoy, Freud, and a company of German neo-romantics.

His comparative analysis of civilizations draws together the insights of earlier German thought. His study of Indian Brahmins, Greek sophists, Chinese sages, and Renaissance polymaths is an attempt to isolate the internal dynamic of social change and to discover what is essentially "western" in Western Civilization.[27] Weber concludes that "the drive for rationality" is the unique characteristic of the West and the source of its modern ascendance. The idea of increasing rationality has its roots in Kant, Hegel, and Spengler. Rationality is a drive for ever-increasing predictability, control, and stability in human relationships, governance, and the physical world.

Most famous is his study of the nature and types of leadership styles. Weber names three—charismatic, traditional, and bureaucratic.

Charismatic leadership is the style of great religious founders. Its legitimacy comes not from tasks performed for followers, but from religious inspiration. The charisma radiates from the leader independent of sanctions, legal arrangements, favors, or special expertise. The great weakness of charisma lay in the difficulty of its passage to a new generation of leadership. The organization which the leader founded would pass to lesser individuals, and the movement would wither away; thus, Weber coined the phrase "the routinization of charisma" to describe the institutionalization of the leader's authority into the next stage of leadership—the legalistic authority of bureaucracy. Thus, bureaucratic authority is power derived from a position. Its occupant needs no special grace, only the visible symbol of office. Finally, traditional leadership is culturally approved and historically venerated power.

Weber's insights are so rich and so numerous that they cannot be summarized here. Even when rejected, they stand as a point of departure for contemporary writers on power.

Soul Force: The Strategies of Non-Violent Power

Mohandas Gandhi (1869-1948), the great apostle of non-violence, was both a theorist and a practitioner of power. His famous "weapon of the weak" is an attempt to overpower a stronger opponent by moving the struggle from the level of physical combat to the arena of moral combat.[28] During this process, both parties undergo a transformation of identity. The weak underdog changes from an outcast to a moral elite. The strong are cast in the role of oppressors and, thus, experience a degree of guilt so intense that they are "converted" to the underdog's point of view. To purge their shame at causing unmerited suffering, they at once surrender their prerogatives and redress the grievances of the weaker party. Of course, events do not always go according to plan. "The fight" scenario has some limitations that will be discussed shortly.

Gandhi fully acknowledged the Anglo-American roots of the conception of non-violent power; however, he treated this heritage as the special contribution of a few very atypical Westerners. Yet, it is probable that the roots of non-violence are as broad and deep in Europe as they are elsewhere. Thoreau and Tolstoy were not the only advocates of non-violence. The British Syndicalists, Sinn Fein, Quakers, Puritan sects of all kinds, as well as women's sufferage and various labor movements practiced non-violence, either as a mode of ethical conduct or as a strategy for successful political action. Gandhi seemed to emphasize[29] one or the other according to circumstances. In times of trouble, he spoke of the intrinsic spiritual merit of the process. At other times, he appealed to the successful results of its application.

Weaknesses of Non-Violent Strategies:

1. Non-violence only works where there is some sharing of values between the two contending parties. Martin Luther King's tactics worked because of the shared Christian heritage between Southern whites and blacks. On the other hand, both Britons and Jews wisely rejected Gandhi's counsels of non-violence against the Nazis. One may overestimate the goodness of human nature or miscalculate the degree of reciprocity of feeling.

2. Non-violence is a misnomer. Because it involves large masses who (without spiritual discipline) could easily become violent, it works as much through the threat of potential violence as through spiritual example. Gandhi had a third of a billion Indians at his back, and he often spoke of what had happened when the crowds got out of control or what could happen in the future. Perhaps, one could say, the non-violent leader is really like Teddy Roosevelt who said, "Speak softly but carry a big stick."

3. The process does an injustice to individuals who may not be guilty of wrongdoing. It lumps all adversary groups together and brands them as wicked. To say that, in every revolution, a few people must be sacrificed is hardly adequate for a strategy with such high moral pretensions.

4. The strategy assumes an identity of interest between the individual and the larger group.

5. A final weakness is that it can be caught up in merely symbolic goals that create a feeling of solidarity but have little real impact upon the fortunes of one's group.

6. It creates a powerful sense of suffering, and, if the movement does not achieve its goals, it may depress the self-esteem of the underdog and make its members feel more like pariahs than ever.

Strengths of Non-Violent Strategies:

1. Because the technique is applied to large masses, it gives a sense of solidarity and belonging to otherwise isolated and despised people.

2. It allows people who cannot participate in the conventional institutional life of the community a chance for direct physical participation. The march was an important activity for Gandhi as it was later to be for Martin Luther King.

3. For the faithful, non-violence provides a religious act and a witnessing of faith. For the more secular, it provides a successful political technique.

Marx, Lenin, Stalin, and other Euro-communists discovered sources of power in technical expertise and in techniques of mass organization. Mao Tse Tung (1893-1978), on the other hand, found it in the fanatical zeal of ignorant masses.[30] The key to power in Asia, according to Mao, lay in the desperation of millions of peasants living in near starvation as they worked tiny, semi-feudal plots of land. What about the urban proletariat so crucial to traditional Marxists? Marx himself felt that the proletariat of his day was the key revolutionary element because of its strategic relationship to the means of production and its relative sophistication about the new industrial order. Lenin began with the belief that power emanated from property alone; the revolution taught him otherwise. Afterwards, Lenin came to rely on the special organizational skills of the party cadres. Stalin relied on technocrats, tractors and the discipline of collective agriculture, and the violence of the party police.

In contrast, Mao turned to the peasants and made a virtue of their ignorance. He called them "poor and blank."[31] The blankness allowed him to write his own messages upon their minds, while their poverty made them desperate—men and women with nothing to lose. This situation made them both steadfastly fanatical in Mao's service and, at the same time, infinitely malleable. Without a stake in the past or leverage on the future, they could become whatever their leader wished them to be. A new message could be written at each stage. For Mao, the revolutionary spirit of the peasantry was a far more decisive weapon than expertise and mechanization.

Of course, it is a commonplace that the different power loci are rooted in the very different experiences of Mao and the Marxist-Leninists. Lenin took power very rapidly, using the urban proletariat and a relatively disciplined party apparatus. Mao, on the other hand, fought two technologically superior enemies (the Chinese Nationalists and the Japanese) in a struggle that lasted many years. It was not with the urban proletariat, but with the peasants who formed the vanguard that he obtained power. His famous phrase "the army swims like a fish in the sea of the peasantry" describes a strategy of using the countryside as his base of operations for both forage, indoctrination, land reform, and recruitment. Only later did he turn to the cities.

After the failures of the Great Leap Forward of 1958, Mao became more than ever estranged from the party apparatus. Born the son of a poor peasant who rose to become a rich peasant and a grain merchant, Mao was sent to school with students of higher status, while his father remained ambivalent about his "classical education." On his part, Mao had mixed feelings about his father's rise. This early attraction to both rebellion and solidarity characterized Mao's later policies. Intellectuals and experts were either being urged to go to the country and learn from the wisdom and virtue of the peasants, or they were being sent there forcibly. Mao frequently declared himself not the master of the peasants, but their most devoted student. While Mao declared that rural laborers were the only group in China to have human worth, he himself spent hours becoming erudite. All his life, he straddled two worlds—the practices of the peasants and the theories of the intellectuals; the lessons of the classics and the mediocre slogans of the revolution, with its elevation of the masses and their ruthless sacrifice for the sake of a new China.

During the early 1960's, the party attempted to "elevate" Mao to an honorary, but godlike, status. By deifying Mao while he was still alive (even Lenin had to wait for death to be turned into a god), they hoped to put him in mothballs as a leader, but retain him as a religious icon. Americans and Europeans who read *The Peking Review* during the early- and middle-1960's saw much evidence of this. Mao Tse Tung's thought was at work everywhere. People performed miracles by invoking his name or reciting his sayings. Story after story appeared of isolated peasants who had performed brilliant surgical operations after repeating inspirational phrases from Mao's little *Red Book*. Once, at a gathering of naval officers, a second sun, a red sun, appeared in the sky directly over Mao. Surely, it was believed, this was a sign that Mao enjoyed the mandate of heaven.

Mao feared that "goulash communism," his phrase for a return to the class system and the consumer ethic that he felt had overtaken the Soviets, would return as soon as the generation who had suffered on the Long March began to pass from power. Thus, he struck savagely at the experts of the party. He unleashed the cultural revolution of 1967 in which the party was crushed between the army and the Red Guards. In the chaos of the ensuing years, he hoped to create worthy successors to the veterans of the Long March. Except for a few of the old experienced cadre, the party, as an effective working organization, was smashed.

In reaffirming the Asian version of communism, Mao denigrated organization and technical knowledge during the years of barely controlled upheaval that followed. The peasantry was established as the sole source of wisdom and legitimacy. Mao, of course, controlled both the peasantry and the army.

The cultural revolution nearly destroyed the university system, crippled industry, and disrupted commerce. Mao was, perhaps, the last Luddite. His cultural revolution produced a bitter reaction. Following his death, Mao was quickly demythologized. His contribution was quickly reevaluated. He was presented as a leader who had outlived his time. The recalcitrant Maoists were denounced as atavistic elements who wished to turn back the clock. In the new China of the 1980's, technology and specialization are firmly in the saddle. The nation has prospered under the new regime nearly as much as it suffered during the implementation of Mao's thought.

Some of Mao's contributions to the literature of power are detailed below:

> 1. "China has 600 million people who have two remarkable peculiarities: they are, first of all, poor, and, secondly, blank. This may seem like a bad thing, but it is really a good thing. A clean sheet of paper has no blotches and so the newest and most beautiful words can be written on it and the most beautiful pictures can be painted on it." *(Peking Review,* No. 15, 19 June 1958, 6).

2. Mao felt that the artist is of crucial importance in mobilizing the masses. The writer or painter takes conflict and makes it typical and abstract. In expressing a typical conflict, however, the artist gives it the form of universal particularity and allows the mass reader to experience it in a vivid way (paraphrase from "Art and Literature in the Service of the People," in *Selected Works,* III, 76-90 passim).

3. Keep volunteerism in the foreground, while terror is always at the ready in the background. Mao believed that the facade of revolution was important. The face of revolution must be the spontaneous smile of the peasant, but the army is always in the background. Thus, the ideology of mass action must be dramatized, carried out, seen, enacted. In this way, the world will see that spirit is more important than expertise or technological devices. (This is not unlike the doomed French doctrine of World War I that affirmed the importance of élan over that of weapons.)

4. Specialization of function must be resisted at all costs and at every turn of the national development. Here, Mao was more communistic than Lenin or Stalin, and far more so than Marx. The role of the bourgeoisie is to be very small and that of the technical expert clearly subordinate. Mao felt that division of labor is the basis of class structure. Specialization creates the base for future stratification and a weakening of the mass base of the movement. [See Stuart S. Schram, *The Political Thought of Mao Tse Tung* (New York: Praeger, 1969), p. 109].

C. Wright Mills and the Power Elite

Jeffersonian, small-town values found a twentieth-century champion in C. Wright Mills (1916-1965), the leading modern theorist of social stratification. Mills had an eighteenth-century suspicion of bigness, of cliques, and of power. A rural Texan who went East to remain a lifelong outsider, his vision of America was the Jeffersonian vision of the arcadian village governed by local sages who jealously guarded its yeoman character and independence.

Mills knew that the America of his childhood was irretrievably lost. Out of this loss, he discovered a sense of mission; he would restore the Jeffersonian ethic in an urban, media-dominated society. As an intellectual, he felt he could play a key role in enlightening the people as to what those in power were up to. Society needs activist-intellectuals. In Mills' view, Jefferson's common people are not doing well. Their liberty has been taken away, and they are no longer able to take hold of their own destiny. The culprits are a group Mills calls "the power elite."[32]

The power elite forms a new ruling class. Composed of interlocking hierarchies of the top military, industrial, and business leaders of America, this class consolidated its power during the national mobilization of World

War II. If the British war experience had brought socialism, the American war experience had seemed to validate corporate capitalism. The new leadership gained access to immense material resources which allowed them to "transcend the environments of ordinary men."[33] Because they consolidated control of so many key institutions, their positions at the top of the pyramid were increasingly interchangeable. Mills notes that generals became university presidents, corporation executives, and politicians. (One example of this horizontal mobility is Eisenhower who, strangely enough to Mills, came to warn of the takeover by the military-industrial complex.) This tremendous centralization of power poses a threat to the autonomy of the individual citizen.

The power of the military elite is virtually unchallenged. Why is this? According to Mills, much of its power is invisible because it is exercised out of public view. Furthermore, it does not rule the citizenry as a tyranny; its acts are covered over with a sugary rhetoric of public-spiritedness and high-mindedness, and rolled in a glaze of egalitarianism. Conspiratorial views have often been popular in America, and Mills' major works, *The Power Elite* and *The Causes of World War III,* outsold all other books in the field of Sociology for more than a decade.[34]

Although Mills' views of power are, at root, American, he had been a student of Marx, and critics note the similarity of his analysis to Marxism. It has been noted that, as Marx's ruling class maintains power by controlling the means of production, Mills' ruling class not only seizes the means of production, but also the instruments of communication as well. Both Marx and Mills value the intellectual and the special insights the intellectual provides.

For Mills, the key personnel of the modern state are the willing servants of the power elite. These are the public relations officers, advertising executives, and the people who either control or have regular access to the mass media. According to Mills, the media masters justify the acts of their bosses through the projection of an image of unselfish meritocracy and democratic public service on their behalf. In fine, Mills' image of America is that of an interlocking power directorate sitting astride an atomized mass society which it controls through advertising and propaganda. The public's view of society is manipulated at its very source. With the aid of the mass media, the power elite has transformed the public into a mass.

Opinion does not percolate up from the masses through the local opinion leaders to be acted upon by regional tribunes of the people. It is insinuated upon the people from the top, while a facade of democracy is maintained through opinion polls (the issues, expression and even phrasing of which have already been determined by the mass media). Under such conditions, the autonomous individual and the Jeffersonian public no longer exist. As a consequence of this, Mills argues, corporate liberalism (his name for the power elite's governance) views these former publics in consumer terms.

People have become passive resources of the power state, not active citizens participating in their own destinies. Unable to shape its own course, the public has become a media market to be manipulated. For Mills, the transformation of the public into the mass means that far fewer people express opinions than receive them; communications are so organized that the individual receiving opinions is unable to answer back with any timeliness or impact; opinion is guided by authorities who dominate the channels of communication; and opinion from the top is seen as the only relevant opinion, so that the masses must initiate a near revolution to have any significant impact on policy (no doubt, Mills would have found an example in the many tax-limiting referendums imposed on state governments in the 1970's).

The role of intellectuals is to form a cadre of dedicated individuals who will help the masses distinguish between their own interests and those of the power elite. These social critics will have "the capacity to shift from one perspective to another, and in the process to build up an adequate view of total life and its components."[35] They will sort out the real issues and, shorn of their technological and ideological verbiage, will pose them in a way that they can be acted upon by laymen in democratic debate.

For intellectuals, the point of attack on the power elite is upon their "vocabularies of motive,"[36] or certain, carefully constructed associations of ideas that form an altruistic facade over the vested interests of various power groups. Thus, the intellectual exposes the glue of self-interest that holds these ideas together and carries on his own war for the dissociation of ideas. According to Mills, under cover of an ideological rhetoric of fear and national defense, it is in the "interest" of the so-called military-industrial complex to foster an association between massive outlays for military weapons and national security. Similarly, it is in the interest of educationalists to foster an association between increased years of education and greater employment opportunities. Mills blames the uncritical public acceptance of the first association for locking us into a never-ending spiral of escalating terror with the Soviets. He feels that perpetuation of the second myth has dealt a heavy blow to humane study. Mills' technique of unmasking power inspired a whole generation of younger sociologists of power who now carry on his work.

John Kenneth Galbraith (1908-   ), a leading political scientist, spent a lifetime studying the nature of power. In his final work on the subject, *The Anatomy of Power*,[37] Galbraith maintains that power emanates from three sources: personality, property, and organization. The power of personality is not only the cult of character or of the great creative individual, but also the use of social conditioning. Although he acknowledges the power of the mass media and advertising in using mass beliefs as a basis for persuasion, he spends little space in the discussion of this important power source. Property was thought by early socialists to be the only source of power differences, and, in the America of the so-called robber barons, automatic power (political, legal, and social) seemed to flow to large propertyholders like Carnegie and Rockefeller. In recent times, organization has become an increasingly powerful source; especially pertinent in this regard is the military. In his study, Galbraith also describes three methods of power enforcement: punishment, compensation, and conditioned power (power by persuasion using appeal to previously held beliefs).

Conclusion

Power is not completely isolatable from its human context, and all attempts to express it as a shorthand mathematical expression point to simple-minded scientism. Power operates within a complex human and environmental situation. Furthermore, much of the time, it is unconsciously exercised, and its use may be both accidental and invisible. Because of its great complexity, it is not surprising that theorists of power (a majority of whom were directly involved in the exercise of power in war, government, or administration) should have come to very different conclusions about this subject.

In the theories we have discussed, there is at least some agreement about the sources of power, but there is rather little agreement about who should exercise power, and even less than that about what constitutes a moral and legitimate use of power. Those who developed a comprehensive plan for seizing and maintaining power show great divergence. With the exception of one or two opportunists, no one supposed that they could isolate a morally neutral use of power.

These fundamental disagreements reflect the different life experiences, personalities, and goals of these thinkers. Some were revolutionaries seeking to destroy the legitimacy of those officially exercising power, while attempting to justify their opportunistic acts as historically necessary. Others articulated ideas that were really defenses of their privileged status as members of a particular class, caste, race, or national group. Still others celebrated ideal visions to create utopian desires for a community yet unborn.

The final chapter will touch on the relationship between power and community.

Notes

[1]For many years, Vold was an advocate of conflict theory in the Department of Sociology at the University of Minnesota. He clashed with Sorokin over the latter's connection between conflict and the incidence of mental disease. Vold pointed out

that, while becoming a mobile system, a class order may expose itself to conflicting values and the envy of other groups. The final result is generally salubrious. Vold stressed that most people enjoy limited conflict and that the consensus-minded sociologists of his time tended to focus only on the negative aspects of competition.

[2]In addition to Plato's dialogues, I recommend A.E. Taylor's *Plato: The Man and His Work,* 7th ed. (London: Methuen Co., 1960); G.M.A. Grube, *Plato's Thought* (London: Methuen Co., 1935; rpt. Boston: Beacon Press, 1958 and 1970). Grube's work is a rich synthesis of Plato's doctrines under various categories. I.M. Crombie, *An Examination of Plato's Doctrines,* 2 vols. (New York: Humanities Press, 1962-1963), contains Plato's concepts of Knowing and Reality.

[3]I refer, of course, to Aristotle's *Rhetoric* (c. 330 B.C.), a book available in dozens of modern translations. It dominated the revival of communication studies in early-twentieth-century Departments of Speech.

[4]Cicero's four collections of letters are *Ad Atticum* (16 books to his close friend, the wealthy banker Atticus), *Ad Familiaries* (16 books to other friends), *Ad Quintus Fratrem* (3 books to his brother, Quintus), and *Ad Brutus.* Cicero's best works on rhetorical theory are *De Inventione* (84 B.C.), *De Oratore* (55 B.C.), and *Brutus* (54 B.C.). His most famous work on politics is *De Republica* (52 B.C.). His most admired speeches ("Pro Quinctio," "Pro Caelius," "Pro Sulla," the "Attack on Verres," and the "Catalinarian Conspiracy Speeches") are available, with many of of his other writings, in the *Loeb Classical Library* (1912-1958).

[5]A biography that places Cicero squarely in the context of his time is that of D.R. Shakelton Bailey, *Cicero: His Life and Letters* (New York: Charles Scribner's Sons, 1971), a scholar whose understanding of Roman politics and whose knowledge of Cicero's letters is unmatched.

[6]David Brion Davis, *The Slave Power Conspiracy and the Paranoid Style* (Baton Rouge: L.S.U. Press, 1969), p. 11.

[7]St. Augustine, *On Christian Doctrine,* trans. by D.W. Robertson, Jr. (Indianapolis: Bobbs-Merrill, 1958), III, i.

[8]Augustine's famous dialogue with his fifteen-year-old son, Adeodatus, is the best statement of his theory of knowledge. See "Concerning the Teacher," in *Basic Writings of Saint Augustine, I,* ed. by Whitney Oates (New York: Random House, 1950), pp. 361-384. The best modern biography of Augustine is Peter Brown's *Augustine of Hippo: A Biography* (Berkeley: University of California Press, 1967).

[9]An account of the interaction between Christian and pagan (Ciceronian) rhetorical tradition is set forth in Gerald R. Press, "Doctrina in Augustine's de Doctrina *Christiana,"* *Philosophy and Rhetoric,* 17 (1984): 98-120.

[10]Niccolo Machiavelli's *Il Principe* (The Prince) and *Tito Livio* (Discourses on the First Decade of Tito Livy) are justly famous and translations abound. Especially good is the Harvey Claflin Mansfield translation (Ithaca: Cornell University Press, 1979).

[11]Thomas Hobbes, *Leviathan* (Modern Library, p. 31.

[12]Ibid., p. 47.

[13]See Richard Weaver's "Edmund Burke and the Argument From Circumstance," in his *Ethics of Rhetoric* (New York: Gateway Books, 1973). Weaver uses Burke's arguments and those of his opponents to illustrate a congruence between form and content. For example, conservatives use a consistent line of argument (definition) as opposed to liberals who draw their conclusions from circumstances. By this test, Burke comes out a liberal.

¹⁴Edmund Burke's "On Conciliation with the Colonies," a speech delivered March 22, 1775, or one day before the famous "Give Me Liberty or Give Me Death" speech of "the Forest-Born Demosthenes" Patrick Henry. There are many nineteenth-century editions of Burke's works, but we lack a complete modern edition. Perhaps the best biography is C.B. Cone's *Burke and The Nature of Politics,* 2 vols. (Lexington: Univ. of Kentucky Press, 1957-1964).

¹⁵Leo Marx, *The Machine and the Garden* (New York: Doubleday, 1954).

¹⁶Those interested in Smith's communication theory will note that Smith delivered lectures on rhetoric and belles lettres at Edinburgh in 1748-1751. See Adam Smith, *Lectures on Rhetoric and Belles Lettres,* ed. John M. Lothian (1963; rpt. Carbondale: Southern Illinois University Press, 1971). See also James L. Golden, "The Rhetorical Theory of Adam Smith," *Southern Speech Journal,* 33 (1968), 214. See also J. Michael Hogan, "Historiography and Ethics in Adam Smith's Lectures on Rhetoric, 1762-1763," *Rhetorica: A Journal of the History of Rhetoric,* II (Spring 1984), 75-91.

¹⁷English translations of most of Hegel's works were published in the late nineteenth and early twentieth centuries, but, apart from those by William Wallace, "Logic" and "Mind" in the first and last parts of *The Encyclopedia of the Philosophical Science,* 2nd ed. (Oxford: Clarendon Press, 1892), they are difficult reading and contain few annotations and notes. Jack Kaminsky's *Hegel on Art* (Albany: State University of New York Press, 1962) is a good summary of Hegel's lectures. Perhaps the most freely available and often translated works are *Philosophy of Right* and *Science of Logic,* trans. T.M. Knox (Chicago: Encyclopedia Britannica Books, 1955).

¹⁸Le Bon's most famous work, *Psychologie des Foules* (Paris: F. Alcan, 1895), translated into English (trans. not identified) as *The Crowd* (New York: Macmillan, 1898).

¹⁹Ibid., p. 131.

²⁰Ibid., p. 125.

²¹A good guide to Marx is *Marx and Engels: Basic Writings on Politics and Philosophy,* Lewis S. Feuer, ed. (New York: Doubleday Anchor Books, 1959).

²²*Marx and Engels: The German Ideology* (New York: International Publishers, 1968). See also Marx, *Capital* (New York: Modern Library, n.d.).

²³In Kenneth Burke, *Philosophy of Literary Form* (New York: Doubleday Anchor Book, 1941).

²⁴See a secret wartime report on Hitler's state of mind by Walter L. Langer, *The Mind of Adolpf Hitler* (New York: New American Library Signet Book, 1973). See also Konrad Heiden, *Der Fuehrer: Hitler's Rise to Power* (Boston: Houghton Mifflin Co., 1944). See Karl Mannheim's translation of *Mein Kampf* (Boston: Houghton Mifflin, 1943), especially Chapter VI "The Significance of the Spoken Word" and Chapters VII and IX on Meetings and Party Organization.

²⁵*Max Weber on Law in Economy and Society,* ed. and trans. by Talcott Parsons (New York: Oxford University Press, 1951), p. 323.

²⁶ See especially "On Charisma and Institution Building," *Selected Papers,* ed. by S. N. Eisdenstadt (Chicago: University of Chicago Press, 1968). See also *The Protestant Ethic and the Spirit of Capitalism,* trans. by Talcott Parsons, 1930 (New York, Scribners & Sons, 1958) and *Theory of Social and Economic Organization* (New York: Oxford University Press, 1947). Do not neglect *Max Weber on the*

Methodology of the Social Sciences, trans. by Edward A. Shills and Henry A. Finch (New York: Harcourt-Brace, 1949).

[27]See *The Religion of India: The Sociology of Hinduism and Buddhism,* ed. and trans. by Hans Gerth and Don Martindale (Glencoe: Free Press, 1955).

[28]A good recent biography of Gandhi is that of William L. Shirer, *Gandhi: A Memoir* (New York: Washington Square Press Pocket Books, 1979).

[29]For an account of his strategy, see his autobiography, *The Story of My Experiments with Truth* (the story of his life up to 1921) and "Satyagraha in South Africa," a pamphlet issued by the Ministry of Information and Broadcasting of India. His collected works, completed in 1958, are in 40 volumes.

[30]An excellent guide to Mao's ideas is Stuart R. Schram, *The Political Thought of Mao Tse Tung* (New York: Praeger, 1961), p. 109.

[31]*Peking Review,* No. 15 (19 June 1958), p. 6.

[32]This is the title of Mills' blockbuster, *The Power Elite* (New York: Oxford University Press, 1956).

[33]Ibid., p. 3.

[34]In 1960, Donald Martindale wrote: "To estimate the significance of his contentions, it is necessary to realize that of his generation Mills is probably the number one sociologist in America," in *Social Life and Cultural Change* (Princeton: D. Van Nostrand Co., Inc., 1962), p. 478.

[35]C. Wright Mills, *The Sociological Imagination* (New York: Oxford University Press, 1959), p. 211.

[36]According to Mills, a motive is a term (or a set of terms and phrases) which appears to an audience to be an acceptable reason for a particular course of conduct. They are idealistic public reasons given to cover up selfish private actions. "Conceived in this way," Gerth and Mills insist, "motives are acceptable justifications for present, future, and past forms of conduct." Thus, when a person describes the reasons for his actions, he is not giving an objective account but "he is ... usually trying to influence others." See Gerth and Mills, *Character and Social Structure* (New York: Oxford University Press, 1952), p. 117 and p. 122.

[37]John Kenneth Galbraith, *The Anatomy of Power* (Boston: Houghton Mifflin Co., 1983).

10

Modern Studies of Communication and Power

The linkage between communication and power was explicitly made by the sophists of fifty-century Greece. Orators like Gorgias and Isocrates celebrated the role of human speech in organizing communities, building institutions, and mobilizing for war. Despite the attractive assumption that language is only a conduit for the neutral transmission of information, modern scholars are almost obsessively aware of the connections between language and social hierarchy. Media advertising has made even ordinary people conscious of the relationship between persuasive messages and human compliance.

One of the simplest and best definitions of power was framed by Bertrand Russell in 1938. He calls it "the capacity to realize our desires."[1] Russell's definition has two major advantages. First, it wisely excludes unintentional manifestations of power and unintended effects. Restricting power to intentional uses is of enormous importance to anyone studying communication behavior. Secondly, Russell sidesteps the behaviorist versus structuralist dichotomy, a dichotomy found in sociological, economic, and political studies of power. Simply put, behaviorists believe that power is widely dispersed (plural) and, thus, they focus on actual transactions. Structuralists, on the other hand, assume that power is concentrated on elite groups who dominate the decision-making process in their communities.[2]

Structuralists study resources and organization. They focus on potential power rather than power in use. Russell's definition encompasses "capacity" (organization and resources) and "realization" (behavior and effects).

Most modern research in power can be grouped under six heads:

1. Autonomous Power (empowerment as a result of personal action);
2. Power as Persuasion (use of rhetorical strategies);
3. Psychic Power (the psychological effects of various power arrangements);
4. Power as Authority (the legitimacy of an agreement or contract awarding the exercise of power);
5. Covert Power (power as manipulation; hidden power; studies of ideology and subliminal seduction);
6. Power as Physical Force (energy in systems; violence).

Only the first five types can be studied from a communication perspective. The remainder of the chapter will review representative studies in each category.

Autonomous Empowerment

The view of autonomous empowerment rejects the belief that individuals are always crushed, dominated, and repressed by power. Here, power is seen as a positive resource. The basic assumptions are as follows:

1. Power is not a finite quantity, but something produced by human transactions;
2. If one individual gains power, others do not necessarily lose it;
3. Acts of cooperation and nurturing can increase power;
4. Power is something that can be generated out of one's own beliefs and actions and through individual reflection and decision.

Peter Adler has framed a theory of momentum as an explanation of individual and group empowerment. The term momentum is frequently used to represent cycles of inspired performance in sports and politics. A politician who wins unexpectedly in one or more primaries is said to have "grabbed Big Mo," and a fumble or interception in football may signal a shift in momentum. Adler sees momentum as "an elite form of behavior."[3] It is a privileged chain of actions, a magical event accompanied by a subjective perception of sudden glory and mastery of one's surroundings.

Momentum feels like divine intervention, but it is precipitated by a real world event. According to Adler, momentum is a socially constructed meaning arising from an initial impetus; hence, "what becomes significant in the transaction process is not whether momentum occurs, but whether or not it is perceived to exist."[4]

Momentum may be seen as a spiraling feedback loop. It begins with the perception of a key event, which must be, in turn, interpreted by the subject as a kind of turning point. This perception has been described in the grandest of metaphorical terms, being called a Janus point, an epiphany, a eureka experience, a godly intervention, a breakthrough from secular to sacred time, the sudden hand of fate, inspiration, and even a special kind of madness. Momentum feeds off successful past action and the continual anticipation of future triumph in a rising tide of feeling. A moment before, the performer, musician, or artist was utterly weak and broken. Then, a single incident triggers a reversal. The subject begins to experience a sense of mastery. The chaotic world grows more coherent. He or she is in control, suddenly able to monitor everything at a glance, and, in a rising tide of brilliant acts, is flooded with godlike power. Momentum is fragile, however, and a sudden disaster can begin a downward spiral of performance and personal disintegration.

A less dramatic and certainly less attractive means of empowerment is found in Charles Derber's study, *The Pursuit of Attention: Power and Individualism in Everyday Life.*[5] According to Derber, attention is a complex of strategies that enhance personal power. Derber records numerous strategies for holding attention and deflecting attention away from others. These include everything from deliberately ignoring the remarks of other people to aggressive interruptions of conversation, subject-changing, civil inattention, giving off boredom signals, and so on.

The use of these techniques is prompted by a kind of atomistic self-promotion, which Derber sweepingly condemns as characteristic of American (primarily male, but increasingly female) discourse behavior. According to Derber, the success formula of marketing (visibility) and the ethic of capitalism have penetrated all other areas of cultural endeavor and are reflected in our patterns of communication.

Burdick and Johns[6], whose work is discussed elsewhere in this book, believe that empowerment comes to individuals who join idiosyncratic or minority groups. While the act of joining such a group may look like an individual surrender of will to outsiders, the joiner may experience quite the opposite feelings. He or she may feel a sense of new freedom, the security to make choices, a rush of autonomous power. The researchers point out that Mexican villagers who join a pentecostal religion quickly become more open to innovation and new ideas than their neighbors who remain Roman Catholics. They become the first to try new agricultural methods, new machines, and new work arrangements. Burdick and Johns believe that the initial act of joining a minority group has set in motion a pattern of risk-taking behavior. Hereafter, even if they should return to the faith of their early years, they will remain forever marked by their decision.

The act of joining a new group gives the joiner a new vocabulary. This new vocabulary functions in two ways. First, it provides a special set of terms, a language in which to conceptualize heretofore ineffable experience. For example, the young soldier to whom the sergeant's advice suddenly becomes meaningful is, at that moment, no longer a civilian, but rather, he has embraced the identity of a soldier. Then, there is the young member of the Neo-Conservative League who finds the leader's sayings (which a day earlier had seemed sanctimonious and silly) to flare up like a nova. Finally, there is the experience of St. Augustine, who embraced Christianity and found writings that had seemed stylistically clumsy and nearly unmeaning suddenly to tap into his deepest realms of experience. Secondly, the vocabulary provides the building blocks for further change. Only the rankest materialists confuse mind and brain. Ideas do not reside in the brain. They are functional and are evoked by social relationships. Language names relationship and perspective and makes them accessible. The movement's vocabulary may sound stereotypical, and outsiders may wonder why a more individual idiom was not chosen to sum up supposedly significant experience, but the repetitive orthodoxy of the words provides a conceptual framework that allows the members to talk about experiences, to critique and refute rivals, to answer critics, and to explore further change.

Finally, the work of William Budenholzer,[7] discussed elsewhere in this text, is important here. For Budenholzer, the act of joining is likened to supplying a formerly missing link in a chain or the missing piece of a puzzle. Powers which have lain dormant for years are suddenly galvanized. Budenholzer's work affirms that groups get that for which they ask. Those that ask little from their members may get nothing. The group that demands everything may get members who are daring, resourceful, and original. Their members will experience emancipation rather than repression. The radical nature of Budenholzer's work lies in the audacity of his claim. He does not speak of a tiny elite, a small core of fanatics, or a mustard-seed cadre. His studies of Viet Cong recruiting convinced him that large numbers of people, at least in some societies, are amenable to totalistic appeals. Those who are asked for a total sacrifice comply with fierce delight. They do so if the stakes are large enough and if there is a world to be won. They have been empowered by a doctrine that gives their personal acts world significance, ideological correctness, and social immortality. In our own experience, people often come together in collectivities which are, usually, mere aggregates of individuals. Even "spontaneous" demonstrations must be staged today.

A coherent explanation of the nature of personal empowerment is obviously several years away. Much of the evidence remains in the form of personal anecdote, narratives of a significant but elusive experience.

Power as Persuasion

Power as persuasion fits an admired Anglo-American model of polity. Political interactions often imply power, persuasion, and influence. Hugh Duncan notes that our nation was born in the midst of forensic drama. Certainly, our Constitution and other founding documents were forged in the crucible of debate. Compared to coercion, mystification, and other modes of allocating power, rhetorical discourse holds a relatively privileged position. For example, we hold certain stock beliefs about the superiority of persuasion. We believe that the breakdown of attempts to persuade is followed by violence; we believe (with Richard Neustadt) that a president's chief power is the power to persuade;[8] we believe that only public debate can forge a policy that is practical, morally acceptable, and effective.

America's greatest rhetorical theorist, Kenneth Burke, sees society as an interdependent series of power groupings or classes who court each other through persuasive discourse. Society is only possible through symbolic collaboration. A vast literature on persuasion in society, among nations, in large organizations, in social movements, in and between groups and dyads exists in the journals of the discipline of Speech Communication.

The work of Max Atkinson[9] attests to the persuasive power of rhetorical form. Atkinson's research (also discussed elsewhere in this volume) proves that a political leader's persuasive power is not solely a matter of good ideas or strategic emotional appeals. He discovered that a small stock of formal devices elicited stormy expressions of approval from political audiences. These stock responses are viewed as public testimony to the speaker's authority and communal certification of a leader's message.

Interest in the relationship between power and persuasion is not confined to Anglo-Saxon countries. Thomas Bates points out, "For all modern Machiavellians, the fundamental categories of power are force and consensus, and they are not mutually exclusive but interdependent...."[10]

Finding the Marxist analysis of power to be inadequate, Antonio Gramsci[11] aims at alternative explanations of social compliance that emphasize communication and de-emphasize economic determinism. According to Marxists, economic arrangements are of primary importance; ideas are largely epiphenomenal. Both Croce and Gramsci posit a two-storied society. A private, voluntaristic cultural realm rises above the public substructure of the Government, the Army, and the Police. The cultural upper story serves as a great clearinghouse for ideas. There, intellectuals serve as spokesmen for rival ideologies, theories, and innovations. Rather than acting as mere consensus builders to supplement the hegemonic power of the state, the intellectuals participate in forensic duel and, thus, operate partially in opposition to the State. The cultural upper story erupts in a battle of interpretations, a vast hermeneutic struggle to determine whose vision of the world will become dominant in a time in which the Great Medieval paradigm has been shattered under the hammer blows of Vulgate translations of the Bible, the rise of many creeds, and the emergence of the capitalist and proletarian orders.

Gramsci sees the future as a vast competition of strident voices, but whose voice is to be the voice of power? Whose voices become the authoritative voices? Who wins the warfare of interpretations? Is it merely he or she who shouts the loudest? Are the voices merely strategic messages? That is to say, have they more to do with the status of a particular intellectual group or the political aims of an elite than with the description of society? Are they the voices of the psychotic that come unbidden from without, voices that have no apparent relationship to the daily environment or daily behavior? No, they are not. Gramsci assures us they could not be endured for a minute if the voices were not useful. They must offer versions of reality that are useful in allowing ordinary people to make sense of their lives and to act in the world.

Important in this regard is the work of West Germany's Jurgen Habermas.[12] According to Habermas, the major institutions of Western Society suffer from a legitimation crisis. Their authority has come under a cloud; they are inherited systems exploited by opportunistic caretakers. Capitalism, Mass Education, Representative Democracy, and all other institutions of social control and socialization must be subjected to intense analysis and discussion. Only public discourse can revalidate them and give discussants a creative experience almost like that of the founders. Of course, this sort of intense forensic participation is, in itself, a process of persuasion. Indeed, the most profound persuasion occurs in extended group participation. The group develops an orthodoxy of participation which must be validated by all its members. The defense of the orthodoxy may, in fact, become as important as its original goals. Habermas advocates a communication behavior he calls "communication competence," a norm that ensures transactions will be at once skillful and egalitarian.[13]

Power as persuasion has been a favorite perspective of those who study communication in the business organization. According to Clifford Geertz, people actively seek meanings in their work, even transcendent meanings. The business organization becomes an arena which people use to make sense out of their lives. Geertz likens people to "spiders suspended in webs of their own meaning."[14]

Paul Olsen concludes that power in business organizations comes to the leader who is able to impose "an acceptable version of what is going on."[15] He further concludes that monetary rewards are inadequate in increasing morale and that the significance of a monetary reward is largely determined by the internal culture of the organization. Thus the role of management is a symbolic one. A manager must assist his or her subordinates in "making sense out of their lives in the organization.''[16]

According to Pfeffer, management is a symbolic action involving ''the construction and maintenance of belief systems which ensure continued compliance, commitment, and positive effect on the participants.''[17] Workers are convinced that their work is vital and important, not just that it fits in somewhere. When the company is in trouble, they must be convinced that their work contributes to the rebirth of the company as surely as the work of the beleaguered executive.

Boston Charlie, the legendary advertising executive, once noted that subordinates engage in imitative behavior, even aping the gait and manner of their managers. He likened the successful manager to the director of a play who must interpret the script, cast the roles, and constantly evaluate the performance. Organizational life must be organized into a sequence of acts that terminate in a meaningful outcome.

Johnny L. Murdock, James J. Bradac, and John Waite Bowers[18] explore the relationship between persuasion and coercion in their study, ''Effects of Power on the Perception of Explicit and Implicit Threats, Promises and Thromises: A Rule-Governed Perspective.'' This work defines power discourse as a ratio of rewards and promises, conditioned by public perception of a speaker's will and resources. Thus, threats and promises (sticks and carrots) have some of the same evidential criteria as persuasive statements in non-coercive situations of free choice. The magnitude of the rewards and punishments must be demonstrated, the credibility of the speaker must be argued, and the probability that sanctions will be used must be defended. On the other hand, flattery, long seen as a primary tool of persuasion by authors of books on winning friends and influencing people, is rejected as weak behavior. In a context of strong coercion, flattery is the behavior of the subordinate.

Psychic Effects of Power

Psychic power is concerned with the metamorphic effects of power on individuals and groups. Many of the students of psychic power have been accused of having a reformist or utopian bias. They have a profound mistrust of large concentrations of power. Like the small-town, Jeffersonian philosophers, they believe too much power corrupts. They tend to condemn institutions and leadership styles that foster powerlessness. They exalt those communication styles that decentralize power.

During the 1960's, a deep fear of the psychic effects of powerlessness on human development was the driving force behind movements concerned with the decentralization of power. Shared power is life-enhancing, positive, and developmental. Denied power is negative, elitist, and stultifying. Participatory democracy was the central vision of many social movements from SDS (Students for a Democratic Society) to the various. Human Emergence movements.[19]

An early landmark work was Abraham Maslow's *Eupsychian Management*.[20] A student of the effects of various power arrangements on workers, Maslow chose participatory democracy as a communication model for his experimental company. Workers were consulted about the business at all levels, decision-making was decentralized, and jobs were expanded to include some dimension of executive-style communication. At the end of the experiment, Maslow came to the same conclusion reached by the Grand Inquisitor in Dostoevski's novel, *The Brothers Karamazov*. The Grand Inquisitor decided that the people were not good enough for Christianity; Maslow concluded that the people were just not up to the level of performance needed to make participatory democracy work. Like genuine Christianity, participatory democracy requires an extraordinary degree of decision-making, energy, responsibility, imagination, and understanding. Despite the modified forms of participatory democracy popular in our airlines (everyone is an executive, steward or stewardess), most practitioners have opted for the modified participation styles of Japanese management. Workers are consulted only at the level of their own competence; thus, a worker who sweeps under machines is asked if the machine is too low or too high for him to sweep under, but he is not asked if the company ought to expand its overseas markets.

David Kipnis has studied the negative effects of various power strategies on human personality. According to Kipnis, certain kinds of power communication corrupt both the holder of power, as well as his or her subordinates. The way in which power is communicated "changes people's view of themselves and of others."[21] For Kipnis, "metamorphic effects" result from the successful application of authoritarian messages:

> If these tactics produce compliance, the power-holder's views of others are changed for the worse. To the extent that power-holders (husbands or wives, politicians or executives) believe that they control another person's behavior, that other person is likely to be devalued. This sets the stage for subsequent exploitations of the less powerful.[22]

Further, Kipnis reports that authoritarian message tactics (giving orders, threats, announcing unilateral decisions) has profound effects for married couples:

> The dominant partners (usually men) also described their companions in less flattering terms in regard to intelligence, success or skill than did partners who shared power.... Dominant partners also expressed less love and affection for their partners and were generally unhappier with the relationship.[23]

If the drive for power has corrosive effects on human personality, it also affects the nature of our organizations and working environments. The studies of Deetz and Kersten[24] suggest that American culture encourages a highly charged political environment characterized by centralized control and manipulated conformity. Americans believe in team spirit. Their deepest belief about organizations is that excellence rests upon conformity. This may account for the climate of constant manipulation one finds in many businesses. Consensus is dearly bought through a fetish of open communication whereby attitudes and ideas are edited down. People feel that they cannot live with diversity. All of the emphasis on esprit d'corps adds up to a mandate for centralized control. This climate may account for the feeling of fatigue and frustration that haunts even creative businesses like advertising where people complain that their ideas have been compromised to the vanishing point.

Power as Authority

In his works, Max Weber teaches us that power is of little use until it is turned into authority. Authority is legitimate power, power that is stable, because it is felt to be right and good to obey it. Thus, a stable leadership class derives power from legitimacy, a right to rule and to keep others from rule. According to Weber, authority is of three kinds: charismatic, traditional, and legal.[25] Charismatic authority characterizes the founding of an organization. The other types are associated with the mature organization. Thus, in Christianity, the charismatic authority of Christ, the founder, is routinized in the priesthood of the church. In the successful organization, the brilliant inspirational leadership of the early years must be embedded in the bureaucratic apparatus of the maintenance years. The shavetail lieutenant is saluted not because of who he is, but because of his rank, an office invested with the full majesty and power of the United States Army.

Legitimacy is social and relational. Richard Newbold Adams[26] writes about the fragility of the relationship. In a democracy, legitimacy comes from the people. If a government does not enjoy majority support, it loses legitimacy. Allocated power is power delegated by the people, and allocated power can be withdrawn. Adams maintains that it is possible to weaken, even cripple organizations as large as nation-states by withholding power. He cites the example of French Canadians, American Blacks, and Palestinian rebels, significant power blocks who have withdrawn some measure of support from their nation-states. He believes they were able to do so because of the very complexity of large groups: "the effect of complexity on allocative power is to make it gradually indistinguishable from the direct exercise of power."[27] Legitimate power always contains some measures of limitation and of reciprocity.

In *The Symbolic Basis of Politics*, Charles Elder and Roger Cobb[28] study cultural premises that can be used to increase governmental mandates. If poverty, crime, and welfare are thought of as personal failings, the government is freed from expectations that it will be able to solve these problems. If, on the other hand, these are defined as structural problems produced by the inequities of the system, the government gains authority over these areas, but also runs the risk that it will lose legitimacy if it cannot meliorate them. Yet, if social problems are defined as personal problems and always addressed at the level of the individual, it will be difficult for rival power structures (countervailing power) to develop.

According to Elder and Cobb, our gospel of self-reliance undergirds a profound suspicion of power:

> Americans have tended to be more impressed by the possibilities for the abuse of political power than they have with the need for political authority. Convinced that "power corrupts," they have not only insisted that political power be fragmented, but they have remained suspicious of the fragments. Even as the expectations of government have grown, Americans have been reluctant to grant it the authority and the resources needed to satisfy these expectations. The results have often been something like a self-fulfilling prophecy, perceived governmental failures serving to confirm the suspicions regarding the untrustworthiness of public authority.[29]

Elsewhere, C. Don Livingston[30] studies the communication environment of authority. His contention is that a rich communication environment tends to be subversive of authority. In fact, political leaders, in particular, claim that too much media reporting tends to wrest control of issues out of their hands (e.g., Media Agenda Setting). Constant media scrutiny places them in a weak reactive posture. Little time is left for reflection or the development of long-range policy. Not only have journalists created a crisis of authority, but they themselves have become the "talent scouts" for new political leadership.

Leslie Gahl[31] studies the ethics of authority. Building on James MacGregor Burns' distinction between transactional and transforming leadership, Gahl comes forward with a new dichotomy: pragmatic versus idealistic leadership. Pragmatic leadership is moved by allegiance to finite, measurable objectives and a sense of duty to a particular constituency. Ultimate leadership is guided by long-range moral objectives. Pragmatic leadership assures legitimacy by defining problems in behavioral terms. Idealistic leadership gains a moral legitimacy through its large vision. It draws its authority from a sense of acting as mediator between the sacred and the secular.

Power as Manipulation

"Brainwashing," "1984," "disinformation," "subliminal advertising," "embedding techniques," and "hegemony" all suggest our fascination with hidden power.

Interest in language as a repository of hidden power has led to a huge number of studies on the subject of verbal dominance. For example, Noelle Bisseret Moreau sees language as the bearer of an "essentialist ideology" that imposes on every individual an identity and a mode of discourse:

> Dominant speech certainly assigns each one her or his place, but only the dominant individuals have the place of singular beings, and, apart from the collection of unique individuals to which they belong, only masses of undifferentiated elements are distinguished "the people" or "Blacks" or "women." Indeed, in the world "order" created and articulated by the dominant, the dominated have no individuality or singularity, and particularities attributed to their group suffice to define them completely.[32]

Again, Muriel Schultz tells us that the "male as the predominant partner has imposed a semantic rule: Male is the norm." This rule implies that so-called universal generic terms such as doctor, lawyer, poet, and editor are not neutral, but include women only as exceptions...."[33]

A related area of study is the embedding of ideology in discourse as a tool of class or group domination. As early as 1964, Murray Edelman wrote, "language contains, expresses and perpetuates the ideologies of those in power."[34] Taking ideology as the transformation of culture into nature, Roland Barthes[35] and other semioticians have invented a visual grammar of graphics in order to expose forms of domination in graphics (television, magazine ads, billboards, etc.), as well as in traditional studies of language text.

No consistent definition of ideology has emerged. Some writers define it as the material relationships between groups, while others refer to it as the expression of relationships of dominance and subordination or the formal justification of particular distributions of power.

The brilliant young scholar, Farrel Corcoran,[36] in "Television as Ideological Apparatus: The Power and the Pleasure," restyles traditional textual criticism to unmask covert domination in the mass media. His self-proclaimed mission is "the decipherment or unmasking of meanings in relation to the overall social formation in which they are encoded or decoded. It (the method) attempts to demonstrate the ways in which mass communication fulfills an ideological mission by legitimating this power structure."[37]

Similarly, Michael McGee[38] has identified the ideograph. These "clusters of slogans characteristic of the collective life" serve as distillations of past ideologies. Thus, "Freedom of the Seas" evokes a great many ideas that have nothing to do with freedom. While such slogans evoke a whole constellation of images and beliefs useful to the patriotic orator, they quickly take on a life of their own.

With incredible daring, Philip Wander,[39] in a landmark article "The Ideological Turn in Modern Criticism," asks communication scholars to examine the ideological underpinings of their own critical perspectives. According to Wander, under the pretense of universality, we may actually serve the established interests of the Anglo-American world view. In a similar vein, Hans Staudlinger[40] warns that scholars of Anglo-Saxon nations with "their outspoken sense for concrete realities and pragmatics do not understand that there exists a revolutionary vision...." He urges us to take "ideology seriously as a blueprint."

On the other hand, some writers downplay ideology. According to Jacques Ellul,[41] we are in the grip of technological determinism. All of our political, religious, and economic institutions have lost their autonomous power. They exist within the framework of technology. Our obsession with technology is reflected in our discourse; technology sets the public agenda and the scope of our discourse. Michael Vickery[42] interprets Ellul to mean that the dominant question is how rather than why.

Finally, Aileen Kraditor[43] suggests that ruling groups have a tendency to project their own values on their constituents; thus, they mistake indifference for alienation.

Conclusion

This brief survey can only touch upon a fraction of the studies done in the area of communication and power. Within the next decade, a swollen torrent of studies will bring the literature of the field to maturity. Then, some genius, a Newton or a Habermas, will impose order out of chaotic and disparate materials. At that time, this mighty sub-discipline will find its place as an autonomous area of study spanning all of the arts, humanities, and social sciences.

Notes

[1]Bertrand Russell, *Power: A New Social Analysis* (New York: W.W. Nórton Co., 1938). Russell defends his definition in the first chapter and develops its scope throughout this work.
[2]Charles R. Spruill, *Power Paradigms in the Social Sciences* (New York: University Press of America, 1981), p. 6.
[3]Peter Adler, *Momentum: A Theory of Social Action* (London: Sage Publications, 1981), p. 177.
[4]Ibid., p. 15.

[5]Charles Derber, *The Pursuit of Attention: Power and Individualism in Everyday Life* (Cambridge, MA: Schenken Pub., 1979), p. 53.

[6]James Burdick and Gordon Johns, *Empowerment and the Act of Joining* (Tucson: unpublished manuscript, 1986).

[7]William Budenholzer, *The Making of a Movement* (Tucson: unpublished work, 1985).

[8]Richard E. Neustadt, *Presidential Power: The Politics of Leadership from FDR to Carter* (New York: John Wiley and Sons, 1980).

[9]Max Atkinson, *Our Master's Voices: The Language and Body Language of Politics* (London: Methuen and Co., 1984).

[10]The best summary of Gramsci's theory of society is found in Thomas R. Bates, "Gramsci and the Theory of Hegemony," *Journal of the History of Ideas, xxxvi,* (April-June 1975), see esp. 356-357.

[11]Ibid., p. 357.

[12]Jurgen Habermas, *Knowledge and Human Interests* (London: Heinemann, 1972), pp. 179ff.

[13]Jurgen Habermas, "Toward a Theory of Communication Competence," *Recent Sociology, No. 2: Patterns of Communication Behavior,* ed. H.P. Drietzel (London: Macmillan, 1970), pp. 369-71.

[14]Geertz, as cited by Paul Olsen, "Making Sense of Sense Making in the Organization," M.A. Thesis University of Arizona 1985, p. 10. For a fuller discussion, see Clifford Geertz, *Local Knowledge* (New York: Basic Books, 1983), p. 61.

[15]Ibid., p. 12.

[16]Ibid., p. 16.

[17]Pfeffer, as cited by Olsen, Ibid., p. 4.

[18]Johnny I. Murdock, James J. Bradac, and John Waite Bowers, "Effects of Power on the Perception of Explicit and Implicit Threats, Promises and Thromises: A Rule-governed Perspective," *Western Journal of Speech Communication* (Fall 1984), p. 44-61.

[19]This insight is derived from Dr. Ernest G. Bormann's lecture, "The New Persuasion: Political Communication in the Age of Media" delivered as one in his series for the *Fifty-Second Annual Distinguished Lectures in Speech,* Louisiana State University, Baton Rouge, Louisiana, September 16-18, 1986.

[20]Abraham Maslow, *Eupsychian Management* (Homewood, Illinois: R.D. Irwin, 1965).

[21]David Kipnis, "The View From The Top," *Psychology Today,* Dec. 1986, p. 30.

[22]Ibid., p. 32.

[23]Ibid., p. 34.

[24]For a critique of Stanley Deetz and Astrid Kersten's position, see Alan Scult, "Meaning and Interpretation in Organizations," *Quarterly Journal of Speech, 72 (1986): 88-113.*

[25]For a discussion of Max Weber that sets his contribution in the perspective of modern organizational theory, see Michael A. Toth, *The Theory of the Two Charismas* (New York: University Press of America, 1981).

[26]Richard Newbold Adams, *Energy and Structure: A Theory of Social Power* (Austin: University of Texas Press, 1975).

[27]Ibid., p. 46.

[28]Charles Elder and Roger Cobb, *The Symbolic Basis of Politics* (New York and London: Longmans, 1983).

[29]Ibid., p. 93.

[30]C. Don Livingston, "An Inquiry into Presidential Leadership Propensity," *Presidential Studies Quarterly*, (Winter 1984), pp. 53-60.

[31]Leslie Gahl, "Moral Courage: The Essence of Leadership," *Presidential Studies Quarterly*, (Winter 1984), pp. 43-52.

[32]Noelle Bisseret Moreau, "Education, Ideology and Class/Sex Identity," in *Language and Power*, ed. Cheris Kramarae, Muriel Schultz, and William O'Barr (New York and London: Sage Publications, 1984), p. 46.

[33]Muriel Schultz, "The Derogation of Women," in *Language and Sex: Difference and Dominance*, ed. B. Thorne and N. Henley (Rowley, Mass: Newbury House, 1975).

[34]Murray Edelman, *The Symbolic Uses of Politics* (Champaign-Urbana: University of Illinois Press, 1964).

[35]Barthes' work is discussed elsewhere in this volume. For the current state of semiotics, see Umberto Eco. *Semiotic and The Philosophy of Language* (Bloomington, Indiana: Indiana University Press, 1984).

[36]Farrel Corcoran, "Television as Ideological Apparatus: The Power and The Pleasure," *Critical Studies in Mass Communication*, 1 (1984): 131-145.

[37]Ibid., 131.

[38]Michael McGee, "The Ideograph: A Link Between Rhetoric and Ideology," *Quarterly Journal of Speech*, 66 (1980): 1-16.

[39]Philip Wander, "The Ideological Turn in Modern Criticism," *Central States Speech Journal*, 34 (Spring 1983), 18.

[40]Hans Staudlinger, *The Inner Nazi: A Critical Analysis of* **Mein Kampf** (Baton Rouge and London: L.S.U. Press, 1981), p. 14.

[41]For a sample, see Jacques Ellul, *Money and Power* (Downers Grove, Illinois: Intervarsity Press, 1984). See also Ellul's *The Meaning of the City* (Grand Rapids, MI: Erdmans, 1977) and Ellul's *Perspectives on Our Age* (New York: Seabury, 1981).

[42]Michael Vickery, a scholar at Northern Alabama University, interprets Ellul to mean that discussion of means is dominant over discussion of ends.

[43]Aileen S. Kraditor, *The Radical Persuasion, 1890-1917: Aspects of the Intellectual History and the Historiography of Three Radical Organizations* (Baton Rouge: L.S.U. Press, 1981). (See esp. her conclusions.)

Index